Teaching That Matters

Praise for *Teaching That Matters*

"*Teaching That Matters* is a delightful concoction of philosophical and psychological reflections and provocations on the art of teaching. Creative teachers will find Frank Thoms's book highly engaging and his practical teaching recommendations enormously useful." —**Hugh Silbaugh**, dean of faculty, Northfield Mount Hermon School

"I feel Frank's energy and commitment and can also hear his voice, literally, as I read. His book feels like a personal conversation rather than a broadcast. Perhaps that is why he was such a good teacher!" —**Ron Stegall**, international education advisor

"I have learned that it doesn't matter whether the students sit in rows, or in pairs, or in a circle on a rug. What matters, and what will engage minds and improve schools is that the teacher in whatever setting is competent, passionate, committed, and willing to take intelligent risks—modeling for students the value of reaching beyond where they are—to where they can be. And in that equation is the role of the principal who must create a culture of respect and trust that supports teachers every day to create rigorous lessons that balance standards with creativity and joy of learning. In *Teaching That Matters*, Frank Thoms advocates close principal-teacher relationships to create engaged learning for students."
—**Patricia Karl**, founder and principal of Lawrence Family Development Charter School, Lawrence MA

"The chapters are so intriguing! I just want to curl up with my favorite plush blanket and spend the day reading what Frank Thoms has written. I love that Thoms understands that one approach to teaching rarely works. He presents multiple ideas and resources to provide teachers opportunities, either individually or collaboratively, to generate their own solutions. And, he offers "Points to Pursue" at the end of each chapter."
—**Pamela Penna**, educational consultant

"Thoms's words invite all readers to come and sit for a spell and soak in meaning through his proactive wisdom and then go out and try it! His book is a page-turner that anyone involved in the profession should pick up and read immediately. As an educator, I was very fortunate to experience his lessons in person and will always appreciate his great leadership and facilitation. Frank Thoms's words and ideas stick, and that is important!" —**Linda E. Ellis**, special education team chair, Gill-Montague Regional School District, MA

"As a fellow teacher, I am not surprised that the lessons in *Teaching That Matters* identify many of today's weaknesses in our education system. In response, Frank Thoms offers exciting and innovative cures, most of which are direct and very doable." —**Frank Gould**, 3rd grade teacher, retired, Enfield, New Hampshire

"It is so important that the wisdom and perspective of a master teacher be shared with the next crop." —**Gael Sherman**, school psychologist, retired

"Frank's commitment to and enthusiasm for teaching is second to none—and he truly gets it. Frank understands that excellent education is the result of teaching which is alive, student centered, and always changing depending on the classroom of learners. He believes that excellent teachers continue to grow and continue to get better every day." —**Rich Perry**, retired principal

"Frank Thoms is one of the rare educators that has the ability to enthusiastically engage learners. As my former teacher, his innovative ways of looking at teaching were inspirational. If you are ready to be inspired, then *Teaching That Matters* is for you!" —**Maribeth Tremblay**, 5th grade teacher, Hopkinton Elementary School, Hopkinton, MA

"Teachers will surely appreciate what Frank Thoms has assembled. His chapters give targeted how-to's without teacher talk. At the same time, Frank presents lively case studies that bring those classroom moments to life." —**Elissa Matta**, StudioStrategize, owner

Teaching That Matters

Engaging Minds, Improving Schools

Frank Thoms

ROWMAN & LITTLEFIELD
Lanham • Boulder • New York • London

Published by Rowman & Littlefield
A wholly owned subsidiary of The Rowman & Littlefield Publishing Group, Inc.
4501 Forbes Boulevard, Suite 200, Lanham, Maryland 20706
www.rowman.com

16 Carlisle Street, London W1D 3BT, United Kingdom

Copyright © 2015 by Frank Thoms

All rights reserved. No part of this book may be reproduced in any form or by any electronic or mechanical means, including information storage and retrieval systems, without written permission from the publisher, except by a reviewer who may quote passages in a review.

British Library Cataloguing in Publication Information Available

Library of Congress Cataloging-in-Publication Data

Library of Congress Cataloging-in-Publication Data Available

978-1-4758-1412-5 (cloth)
978-1-4758-1413-2 (pbk.)
978-1-4758-1414-9 (electronic)

To my dear friend and colleague, Barbara Barnes, whose listening, advice, and wisdom inspires me to reflect about my teaching and to write about it

In memoriam Christina Ward, 1953–2012, my first editor, wise counselor, and dear friend

"When you grow up you tend to get told the world is the way it is and your life is just to live your life inside the world. Try not to bash into the walls too much. Try to have a nice family life, have fun, save a little money.

That's a very limited life. Life can be much broader once you discover one simple fact, and that is—everything around you that you call life, was made up by people that were no smarter than you. And you can change it, you can influence it, you can build your own things that other people can use.

The minute that you understand that you can poke life and actually something will, you know if you push in, something will pop out the other side, that you can change it, you can mold it. That's maybe the most important thing. It's to shake off this erroneous notion that life is there and you're just gonna live in it, versus embrace it, change it, improve it, make your mark upon it.

I think that's very important and however you learn that, once you learn it, you'll want to change life and make it better, cause it's kind of messed up, in a lot of ways. Once you learn that, you'll never be the same again."

—Steve Jobs. "One Last Thing." Pioneer Productions, PBS, 2011

Let life change you. —Scott Simon

Dear Reader,

The book you have in front of you, *Teaching That Matters: Engaging Minds, Improving Schools*, offers a compilation of invitations to improve teaching practices. You will discover a series of ideas and approaches that will invigorate schools and classrooms. Whether you work in education or are a citizen concerned about the future of schools, this book invites you to participate in this important conversation.

In countless classrooms where students sit at desks in rows, you will see teachers who appear not to be involving students. But if you look carefully, you will find other teachers extending themselves to engage them.

At the end of the second-floor hall, Peter Travis, a young language arts teacher, begins to deliver yet another lecture from behind his podium but suddenly puts down his notes, pulls a chair to the side of the room, sits down, and begins to ask his students provocative questions.

He wants to hear what they have to say about his previous three lessons. He listens and after each comment, he waits. When the discussion slows, Peter asks, "What questions do you have?"—not "Do you have any questions?"—as he's discovered recently that he gets more and better responses from the first question.[*]

In the principal's office at the same high school, Dan Birch ponders his faculty's obsession with the school's testing program. He observes that too many of his teachers focus on test prep rather than encourage students to think and create. In a recent conversation with his assistant, Joyce Barnes, he finds that he likes the idea she shares about the Golden Toilet Award, which she discovered at a conference. The award is given to any teacher who takes a risk to try something new and then fails.[**]

Dan thinks, "Why not introduce this idea at the next faculty meeting and, at the same time, share my idea of publicly recognizing teacher successes?" He feels that for too long what happens in classrooms stays in classrooms. Dan is eager to shift the school's culture toward a more open, more collaborative atmosphere.

Down the same hall from Peter Travis, Margaret Rivers, a veteran social studies teacher, decides to try an idea for her geopolitical class that she learned from a colleague. Before her students arrive, she places a sign in each corner of her room: "Agree," "Strongly Agree," "Disagree," "Strongly Disagree." On the board she writes:

> Upon closer examination, Russia's gigantic size has been overestimated. For all practical purposes, it is really a small country.
> —M. T. Smallbigovich, Soviet Geographer, University of Moscow

For the past two weeks, Margaret's students have been intrigued about Russia's complex history, its vast landscape, its arctic orientation, and its dwindling population. She asks students to choose the corner of the room that reflects their position on Smallbigovich's statement.

She wants them to take a public stand, debate with each other, and be open to change the corner they chose, based on evidence offered by classmates. Simply by standing up, their thinking should be stimulated, especially after lunch—something she learned from brain research.

Peter Travis, Dan Birch, and Margaret Rivers represent the intention of this book. You will meet other teachers and administrators who take steps to make schools safe and challenging. You will see each of them as a risk taker. Each takes the initiative to stimulate student learning. Each chooses to seek new and better ways to reach today's digitally wired students. Each knows that engaged learning in class increases chances for retention and understanding. And, each knows schools that foster safe communities and rigorous teaching nourish students' gifts and strengths. You are welcome to join them on their journeys.

Frank Thoms

NOTES

* Ted Thornton made this important distinction at a faculty workshop at Northfield Mount Hermon School, January 5, 2011.
** Robert Evans, (2001), "National Seminar for the Experienced Pro," Mallery Seminars, Philadelphia, Pennsylvania.

Contents

Foreword		xv
Introduction		xix

I: Re-Imagine Teaching
1	Confidentiality: End Classroom Isolation	3
2	Dialogue: Build Teacher-Administrator Relationships	9
3	Coaching: Provide Nonjudgmental Teacher Support	15
4	Lessons: Create Ambiguity to Stimulate Thinking	21
5	Conversation: Make Time for Reflective Talking and Listening	29
6	Research: Bring Brain Research Into the Classroom	39
7	Sabbaths: Take Occasions to Turn Off Electronic Devices	51
8	Symphony: Teach to the Whole Child	63
9	Recruit: Make Schools Safe for All Students	71

II: Seek New Perspectives
10	In the Classroom	77
11	Beyond the Classroom	95

III: See Things as They Are
12	Purge PowerPoint: See the Emperor Without His Clothes	113
13	Everything Has Its Own Speed: Don't Kill the Butterfly	119
14	The Four Agreements: Find Your Center	125

IV: Write Letters
15	Letter to Alicia: Celebrate Your Uniqueness	135
16	Letter to Peter: Be Yourself	141
17	Letter to Pamela: Make Relationships Your Priority	147

V: Build Trust and Respect
18	Replace Factory Model Schools: Eliminate Debilitating Hierarchies	157

19 Invoke a New Paradigm: Make Trust and Respect the
Centerpiece of Schools	163

Epilogue	169
Index	171
Acknowledgments	181
About the Author	183

Foreword

Working as an educational administrator for over thirty years, I was never able to have dessert. I led with the appetizer, the endless planning meetings in preparation for major initiatives we were about to unveil. I partook of the entrée, as well, the implementation of the initiatives, observations, data gathering, and the resultant endless tweaking.

But I was never able to savor the dessert, the celebration of what my colleagues and I accomplished for students, parents, and teachers. Because of the demands of the appetizers and entrees, I could not enjoy the fruits of success. I was on the way to burnout.

Until I met Frank Thoms.

Frank became my ally on the pathway to the dessert I so needed. I first met him in 2000 as a new assistant superintendent. At that point in my career, I had been a teacher and principal for almost twenty-five years in both public and private schools. Without ever having my dessert, I worried about sustaining my enthusiasm as a central office administrator.

In my new district, I became responsible for the professional development of teachers. When Frank arrived, we shared stories, mine about my administrative career, his about his passionate years in the classroom. Together we assessed the needs of the district and drew up plans. The longer we worked together, the more I could begin to smell the dessert. Frank helped me understand what works and what does not, and that success is not an accident.

We developed a series of workshops and courses for the district's new teachers, mentors, and veteran staff. He designed innovative programs tailored to our curriculum needs. He also delivered keynotes at the beginning of the new school year. He became a friend and confidant to our teachers.

When I moved on as an administrator in other districts, Frank and I maintained our relationship. We planned courses, workshops, and keynotes. For the past ten years, I have been a superintendent and have kept close ties with Frank. He has implemented innovative programs in differentiated instruction, standards-based curriculum, new teacher workshops, classroom management, workshops on standards for high school faculty—and led Socratic-style seminars for me and my administrative team.

For what seems like over one hundred hours of collaboration in classrooms, in schools, over the phone, at workshops, and even dinners in restaurants when there was no room left in the work day, Frank helped me become a better educator. Now in my work where I still provide the appetizer and the entrée, I can now enjoy the dessert. I maintain my zest and vitality for what some call "God's work."

And that's what this book is all about: maintaining the same wondrous curiosity for learning, for ourselves as well as for our students, which makes the acquisition of knowledge, skills, and understandings—and a love of learning—the real dessert of life.

Frank Thoms was gifted early on in his career with an understanding about what matters in teaching, what most of us do not realize until our teaching careers are nearly over. Because the task of teaching is so complex, we plow forward with our heads down and miss the forest for the trees. For many of us, our eureka moment arrives as we decide to start moving up the administrative ladder, or unfortunately for others of us, as we leave education altogether.

Frank discovered his first eureka moment in his second year of teaching. At that time, most teachers were teaching from a podium at the front of the room, where students sat in rows and were allowed virtually no opinion or options regarding what would take place during the lesson. These teachers created over ninety percent of the sound in the classroom.

In his social studies classroom, Frank brought student learning to a much higher level beyond simple recall. He knew he was breaking new ground. Some colleagues greeted his experiments with great skepticism. In his introduction, Frank gives superb examples of his ingenuity throughout his nearly forty-year career in catalyzing students to high levels of creativity. He consistently asked students to become more responsible for what happens in the classroom—and for their own learning.

Despite school reform efforts in the past one hundred years, significant bastions of resistance still allow students to fail because they are just plain bored and unmotivated. The most egregious resistance is the inability of many schools to recognize the cultural changes that have arisen from the explosion of technology in the culture. Yet, like it or not, digital technology is washing over our schools and classrooms.

Some districts have dumped textbooks entirely and substituted them with notebooks, laptops, and iPads. Here Frank is again ahead of the curve. In his introduction, Jim McMillan, who changes the landscape of his classroom, understands the role of the teacher as facilitator in the electronic age. He perfectly sets the stage for the book.

I would make Frank's chapter, "Sabbaths: Take Occasions to Turn Off Electronic Devices" required reading for all teachers and administrators. In this chapter, we learn that we must make our peace with the fast-changing digital culture—and in fact embrace it. Yet, at the same time we must understand that it cannot become the tyrant that dictates what we do in the classroom.

Just like the old blackboard and chalk, Frank respects digital devices as tools. Many of us have heard the expression that God speaks to us when there is silence. When we choose to turn off electronic devices, we allow our innate intelligence and creativity to speak to us as lifelong learners.

Teaching That Matters: Engaging Minds, Improving Schools matters. It matters to teachers and administrators. It matters to educational planners, like state legislators steeped in accountability who, in their insistence on nonstop assessments, forget what most students need. And, it matters to students who deserve an engaged education.

We need to help students make sense of our educational system and understand why they are there. We need to help them appreciate school as a collaborative place where they have a role in what and how they learn. We need to show them that reaching their highest educational potential is a function of being able to have choice in what they do in the classroom — and that learning is indeed the dessert of life.

Anthony T. Polito
Superintendent of Schools,
Athol-Royalston Regional School District

Introduction

Teaching is an enormously complex activity.

It means to spend each day with thirty or more students in a classroom. It means to be responsible for their learning and behavior; listen to their complaints; celebrate their successes; and commiserate in their failures. It means to respond to angry parents; cope with administrative pressures; keep pace with curriculum demands; prepare to meet outside assessments; design units of study; create lessons; give quizzes, tests, papers, and projects; and toward the end of the day take care of family matters—and before retiring, correct tests and papers and prepare lessons for the next day.

Inside the complexity of teaching, schools are best served by those teachers who move beyond traditional patterns of teaching solely from the front of the room and work alongside their students. From my first years in the early 1960s I chose to be an innovative teacher. In my second year at a junior-senior high school, when I moved from the ninth to the eighth grade, I decided to teach Marxist-Communism from the inside.

After pulling the shades on my windows and blocking the clear glass panel on my door, I spent a week practically preaching the virtues of Marxist-Engels principles. Using stick-figure diagrams and holding volatile question-answer sessions, I invited my students to internalize the virtues of the enemy's ideology. I reinforced it by having them spend a day dressed up in Soviet-school garb and emulate learning the Soviet way. It was a remarkable time.

Ten years later, after a year of teaching in an exemplary Oxfordshire, England, open-plan progressive primary school, I returned home to establish a sixth-seventh-eighth-grade open classroom. I was fascinated with the idea of working with fellow teachers to provide opportunities for students to become drivers of their own education—inside our rigorous expectations.

For social studies, I took the board game "Diplomacy"[1] that had been designed for two to seven players and made it into a class-wide simulation activity involving twenty-plus students that lasted more than a month. The simulation was complete by having "diplomats" engage in intensive negotiations before making moves on the board; creating multiple "alliances" between countries; making secret "agreements"; and preparing "propaganda" posters that were scattered throughout the classroom.

The game concluded with a Diplomacy dinner, in which students (most of whom were not involved in the game) designed a menu based on different European cuisines and did all the cooking and serving.

Another innovation from that time was my restructuring the board game "Monopoly" into a socialist version I called "Co-opoly." The rules specified that players were to play to win an equal share of money and real estate. It was a struggle for my students but proved intriguing. I wish I had kept a copy of the rules.

Later, in the mid-1980s when I taught social studies as a member of a more traditional team of four teachers, I again revisited U.S.-Soviet relations. Gorbachev's *glasnost* was tempting Americans like me to travel to the Soviet Union and to see the "enemy" behind the Iron Curtain. I ended up taking eight trips, on three of which I served as a teacher of English in Soviet schools in Leningrad and Alma Ata, Kazakhstan.

In my classroom at home, I wanted my students to see Soviet history as realistically as possible. Propaganda from both sides was rampant. I decided to use George Orwell's *Animal Farm* as a way into the Soviet mind and its modes of operation. A remarkable feature of the book is that Orwell never mentions Russia or the Soviet Union.

My students read one chapter per night, followed by class discussions the next day. I convinced them not to read ahead so we could speculate on what might happen. After finishing the book, the *pièce de résistance* was offering students the option to reenter the book at any part and rewrite it in a way that they saw fit.

One of their favorite choices turned out to be "Chapter XI," a postscript to Orwell's final chapter, "Chapter X" with its infamous quotation: "The creatures outside looked from pig to man, and from man to pig, and from pig to man again; but already it was impossible to say which was which."[2] The futures that students envisioned may not have satisfied Orwell, but they did represent original thinking in often well-written essays.

My final incarnation teaching about Russians and the Soviets happened with eighth graders in a private school in the 1990s, my last decade in the classroom. As part of our study, we spent considerable time examining the plight of peasants during the reign of Ivan IV. I asked students to take roles in Russian society and draft petitions on behalf of peasants to present to the tsar.

After thorough research and intense class discussions, including pouring over texts written by Edward L. Keenan at Harvard, students prepared authentic-looking parchment petitions laced with burnt edges. When they delivered their petitions to Ivan IV, a colleague disguised as the tsar, they approached him reverently and dropped to their knees. The combination of authentic-looking petitions, well-researched information, and dressing as peasants and nobles to face the tsar—and never turning their backs on him—put them deep into early Russian history.

These examples of breaking the traditional pattern of teaching solely from the front of the room illustrate that teaching can be a creative process with endless possibilities. By no means did I limit myself to Marxism-Communism, Russian History, and the Soviet era. Throughout my career in whatever grade or subject, I engaged students' minds, encouraged them to do their best, and invited them to express their knowledge in rigorous and creative ways. It was the only way I knew how to teach. It's the reason I write.

~ ~ ~

Inside the whirlwind of today's schools, Jim McMillan, a flamboyant middle school math and science teacher, is well-known for his innovative use of a SMART Board: an interactive whiteboard that connects to his computer, writes notes in digital ink, and saves classwork for absent students who can access it from their computers at home—all with the simple touch of his finger.

Jim puts relentless pressure on himself and on his students to perform well. He knows that he has to meet outside expectations, often beyond his capacity, often without enough time, enough materials, and enough support. He feels this pressure every day. And it escalates when students disrupt, act out, or fall asleep.

When visitors step into a hallway at Jim's school during the change of classes, they are overwhelmed by the cacophony of voices and movement. At the bell, students burst from the quiet of their classrooms. These three minutes fashion a momentary counterculture, one which the visitors may well remember from their high school days.

Jim and many of his colleagues are aware that their students live increasingly complex lives. They hardly have time to themselves. Homework takes a backseat, as social media demand constant attention. Early-morning classes barely keep them awake, as late-night texting intrudes on their sleep. Afterschool jobs for some demand as much time as school; sports, and lessons and clubs overfill time for others. Countless students return home to empty houses; many eat supper alone. They are grateful for their cell phones and computers. Facebook "friends" replace friends.

Amid these cultural changes, Jim has noticed that colleagues still hold onto embedded practices. They stand and talk at students sitting quietly at desks. They teach from old notes. They're unwilling to try new technologies.

Several of Jim's math colleagues still start the first fifteen minutes of class by having students volunteer to put their homework problems on the board. They tediously review each problem and conclude with the seldom answered, "Does anyone have a question?" For the next twenty minutes, they review material for the next lesson right out of the book—maybe the class tries one or two problems together. For the last fifteen minutes, students start the homework while the teacher either circulates to help or remains at her desk to prepare for the next day.[3]

Not true for all of Jim's colleagues, not true in every classroom certainly. Still, these old methodologies prevail. Ask any student.

Jim believes that change, any change, remains difficult for most people, especially teachers. He remembers his early years when he discovered his natural inclination to look for new ways to teach. He intrigued his students whenever he could find alternatives to textbooks. Now that his new science course will require more lecturing, he wants to incorporate "10-2 thinking" (talk for ten minutes, give students two minutes to process what he's told them, then repeat this pattern throughout his lecture).[4]

When he first learned of this technique, it made obvious sense to him. However, he was surprised at his colleagues' resistance to try it. Jim thinks that many of them prefer to stay with the familiar, even when they know that they could do differently or better. Routines keep them safe. They are creatures of habit. They do not want to unravel their comforts.

Yet, while Jim has observed that many colleagues stand at the front of the room, it does not mean they are poor teachers. Some of them create an enrapturing presence. His friend and high school colleague, Peter Smythe, who prefers to wear jeans and open-collared shirts, stands behind his podium nearly every day. He delivers dynamic interactive history lectures that enthrall his students and create indelible memories. His students learn how to engage in active listening, an essential skill for both school and life.

However, Jim worries about other colleagues who hide inside cocoons of old practices that don't command attention, don't invite curiosity, and don't create memories. They repeat boring routines, dole out lessons that barely feed the mind, and give assignments that fail to inspire.

Jim McMillan knows that the landscape of schools and classrooms are undergoing rapid fundamental changes. Now in his twenty-first year of teaching, he recognizes that technology and its natural derivative, digitally wired students, are confronting traditional textbook-driven curricula. He already intends to eliminate textbooks, as he knows that he and his colleagues can no longer count on using them as they used to. Teachers, Jim believes, need to be inventive in response to the new and fast-changing culture.

Curious as to the potential impact of the Internet on his teaching practice, Jim often searches for new approaches. One evening, he explores Khan Academy's open-web access to rich materials and innovative approaches for learning math. He's fascinated with the idea of having his students learn on their computers at home *before* coming to class and then processing the material with Jim *during* class. After exploring the idea with his students, he decides to experiment using the Khan Academy's approach with his eighth-grade pre-algebra class.

After a month, Jim is convinced that this class is more engaged and is retaining material better than his others. He decides, then, to implement the Khan Academy approach with all of his classes, yet he knows that some students will resist, as they have been used to teachers delivering lessons.

Now that all of his classes follow the Khan Academy system, Jim no longer *delivers* math lessons but instead takes on the role of *facilitator*. He attends to what his students have learned (or not) from the previous night's Khan Academy lesson. He provides opportunities for them to process, clarify, and evaluate their new knowledge. He's able to interact with them nearly every day.

Jim enjoys spending more time interacting than presenting. His students are retaining the material better. Still, for some this approach remains a struggle, as they prefer the old way. After much personal conferencing, he convinces his reluctant students to stick with him on this approach, as he knows that he's onto something. He's delighted at the academy's comprehensive offerings, sequenced curriculum, positive attitude—and versatility.

~ ~ ~

The decision to make teaching better does not happen on its own. It happens when principals, teachers, parents, concerned citizens, and students make the effort. Impetus to improve classroom life comes from multiple sources.

For instance, a teacher becomes dissatisfied with the lack of class participation, so he readapts his pedagogy to enable him to hear more from his students and less from himself. A middle-school principal sees an opportunity to encourage an eighth-grade science teacher to convert her classroom into a learning laboratory instead of a knowledge filler.

A school head moves a reluctant teacher to a different grade, which surprisingly gives him a renewed sense of teaching. A parent invites a teacher to take inspiration from the film *Stand and Deliver* in which Jaime Escalante succeeds in having all his East Los Angeles High School students pass the AP Calculus exam. And, a fifth-grade teacher becomes inspired by a writer whose book and blog taps into her desire to learn about better strategies that will engage her students.

Teaching That Matters: Engaging Minds, Improving Schools invokes the knowledge and wisdom of teachers like Jim McMillan who give educators and concerned citizens multiple ideas from multiple perspectives. In the spirit of Steve Jobs, the book, through the voices of innovative teachers and principals, provides diverse ways to "think different" about practice. These educators offer imaginative approaches to "poke life" in schools and classrooms.

Taken together, the chapters offer a smorgasbord of best practices. Each one plants seeds that lead to making teaching better but leave open the choice of road maps as to how to get there.

Ultimately, the destiny of a great education depends upon the participation of whole communities in which everyone commits to make learning successful for all students. Implementing changes in schools hinges on what teachers and administrators *choose* to do. It begins in the classroom.

NOTES

1. Diplomacy (Games Research, 1961).
2. George Orwell, *Animal Farm* (New York: Harcourt, Brace and Company, 1946), 118.
3. With thanks to Bob Milley who reminded me of this pervasive pattern in math classes. My stepson, who was attending an elite private school, experienced exactly that same pattern in his ninth-grade algebra class for advanced math students—and spent half the year reviewing the previous year.
4. Mary Budd Rowe introduced the concept of 10-2 in 1983!

I

Re-Imagine Teaching

> That is the way you learn most, that when you are doing something with such enjoyment that you don't notice that the time passes.
> —Albert Einstein, in a letter to his son Albert

When teachers imagine ways to become better, they release themselves from the grip of embedded traditional practices.

Part I offers nine different perspectives for improving teaching.

To re-imagine teaching opens possibilities for creating engagement in the classroom. When teachers choose to re-imagine, they begin to let go of the mindless replication of embedded practices that have outlived their usefulness. They begin, too, to invite administrators and students to become active participants in their classrooms.

Each chapter in part I suggests rather than insists but nonetheless brings important issues to the forefront. Each acts as a seed to encourage rethinking the teaching process. The first chapter addresses the isolation of the classroom; it argues that strong mentor–new teacher relationships can break open this isolation and develop serious collegiality and creative collaboration.

The second chapter redefines the teacher-supervisor relationship, one that moves away from the dog-and-pony-show model and in its place creates mutual trust and respect between both parties.

The third chapter invites teachers to improve practice by welcoming honest feedback from colleagues and coaches. The fourth focuses on designing lessons that are less linear and more open to ambiguity to nurture thinking.

The fifth chapter introduces Margaret Wheatley's six principles for open conversations that invite teachers to re-imagine the power of listening in the classroom. The sixth chapter encourages teachers to incorporate proven ideas from brain research to increase opportunities for students to learn what they need to know, understand, and be able to do.

The seventh reaffirms the essential joy of face-to-face lessons, which free teachers and students from the constant chatter of electronic devices—and anxiety from their silence.[1]

The next-to-last chapter in this section asks teachers to pay attention to the whole person inside each student; if, instead, they only teach how to take tests, students will be shortchanged—and so will teachers. The last chapter advocates Robert Kegan's profound idea that school staffs recruit every student so that none of them remain anonymous.

When educators choose to re-imagine teaching, they do not settle for what they do every day. They become open to insights, surprises, stumbles, twists, and possibilities on how to engage students and themselves.

NOTE

1. Throughout the book I make references about the distraction and tensions from ever-present electronic devices. Much of the clarity of my arguments is supported by Sherry Turkle's impeccable research, particularly Part II, "Networked: In Intimacy, New Solitudes" in *Alone Together: Why We Expect More from Technology and Less from Each Other* (New York: Basic Books, 2011). (For an excellent distillation of her arguments see Sherry Turkle, "The Flight From Conversation," *New York Times, Sunday Review: The Opinion Pages*, April 21, 2012, at: http://www.nytimes.com/2012/04/22/opinion/sunday/the-flight-from-conversation.html?pagewanted=all&_r=0.

ONE
Confidentiality: End Classroom Isolation

The choice to form "Critical Friends Groups"(CFGs) enables mentors and new teachers to move beyond their confidential relationship and improve teaching and learning—not only for themselves but also for their colleagues.

Increasing numbers of school districts recognize the importance of assigning mentors to shepherd new teachers (protégés) through their first three years. Some offer mentor training programs for veterans. Pam Peters, a well-respected, experienced teacher trainer for fifteen years, has had multiple opportunities to run such workshops.

Among the required topics that she and her colleagues bring up at every workshop is the sacred role of confidentiality between mentor and protégé. What happens between them stays with them. To give confidentiality its due, she, as she usually does, brings it up near the end of the workshop:

"Please turn to page 26 in your packet and read the following statement about confidentiality."

1. Mentor teachers will be able to discuss, in confidence, any aspect of their protégé's performance with other members of the mentoring team.
2. Mentors, with the protégé's knowledge and permission, may discuss the protégé's teaching performance with resource professionals whose job it is to help teachers. (For example, if the novice needs help in designing hands-on science lessons, the district science coordinator may be consulted for help and advice.)
3. Mentors, with the protégé's knowledge, may discuss the protégé's teaching performance with appropriate administrators if, in the

mentor's professional judgment, the academic growth and development, social wellbeing, or physical safety of the students is at risk.

> "As you can see," Pam says quietly, "these three principles form the heart of a confidential relationship. We think that they assure that protégés will feel confident that you will have their back at all times. Be sure that you are clear about them. What questions do you have?"

In the conversations that follow, participants quickly agree to keep this confidentiality. When Pam brings up the issue of how to talk to the principal when he asks about their relationship with their protégé (e.g., "How's it going with the new teacher?"), they immediately grasp her suggestion to respond with a nondescript comment in a respectful manner, such as, "Just fine, thank you." They clearly understand that confidentiality is key to the mentor-protégé relationship, except when students are compromised.

One evening as she reflects on this confidential relationship, Pam wonders if it has an unintended consequence of furthering the perpetual isolation of classrooms.

> "Maybe, that's why mentors in workshops rarely question this aspect of mentoring. After all, as I used to do, teachers often regale about their classrooms as their own world. As students enter, they close their doors and say, 'Welcome to my world' or something similar."

As a new teacher a generation ago, Pam clearly understood that her classroom—Room 22 across from the main office—belonged to her. No one came in unless she knew beforehand. It was the way it was, and the way her colleagues believed it should have been.

She, like many of her colleagues, loved that world. She took great pride in making her classes exciting and innovative. But she often wondered about those teachers who simply put in their time and followed the pages of the textbook, lectured every day from old notes, never collected homework, and even failed to return papers.

These teachers, Pam imagines, could have been the teacher in the movie *Teachers*, who puts his feet up on his desk and reads the newspaper in every class throughout the day. His students arrive sheepishly and obviously intimidated, take worksheets from trays, fill them out at their desks, and return them at the bell. Later in the film he's discovered in the same position at his desk after being dead for several days.[1]

Given that teachers teach alone and are rarely observed, how do people know what actually happens in classrooms? What *is* the teacher doing? What *are* the students doing? In recent years in some states, high-stake tests determine whether students are considered successful or not. So far, few teachers are held accountable for the failures (or successes) of their students, in part because the test results come long after they have moved on. This may soon change.

Shirley Martin, a fourth-grade teacher for more than twenty years and known for her quirkiness, sense of humor, wild gesturing—and long skirts—enjoys learning about new ways to teach. Recently, she returned from a conference in which she learned about Critical Friends Groups. She could hardly wait to tell her protégé, Ann Rodriguez, about this idea.

Ann already demonstrates a curiosity about new ways of teaching. She has lively ideas. Some work, some don't. She relates well to her students, listens to them more than most of her colleagues, and is open to Shirley's feedback. When Shirley shares her excitement about the conference, she suggests to Ann,

> "Why don't we open our doors to each other throughout the day? You and I have a good relationship and could certainly benefit from learning first-hand about each other's teaching styles. And why don't we invite other teachers into our classrooms? At the conference, I learned about the idea of teachers opening doors to one another—'to go public' with their teaching— a concept that has been practiced for more than a dozen years albeit in only a few schools."
>
> Shirley added, "And, I know a sure-fire way to pique the interest of our fellow teachers. We will show them 'Looking at Student Work: A Window into the Classroom,' a film that I bought at the conference." She then describes a key segment of the film:
>
> "A group of teachers and a facilitator, who have been meeting as a Critical Friends Group, gather around a large table to discuss student work within a strict-timed protocol. In the clip, Al, a business education teacher, expresses his concern that his students have done poorly on his exam; none of them did better than a C. He explains the structure of the exam and passes out sample copies.
>
> Then, Friends, fellow teachers in his CFG, ask him clarifying questions. He answers them and then sits back. He listens with comment as the facilitator and Friends discuss his concerns among themselves and offer ways to improve his exam. After they finish, the protocol allows Al the opportunity to share his impressions of their ideas. He does— and he expresses his gratitude. The group then debriefs.[2]
>
> Taking a breath, Shirley continues, "After we saw the video, we had an opportunity to carry out a similar but shortened protocol role play. We were surprised at how much we liked its structure, as the conversation focused on student work, not on us as teachers. We all agreed that this practice would benefit our teaching. Most of us, however, were skeptical about winning administrative support or finding time in the school day to make it happen."

Once Shirley and Ann share the video with their grade-level teaching team, they invite them along with Mark Harris, a vice principal whom they like and respect, to form a CFG. As Friends, they first meet during a regular planning time; later, they decide to meet after school so they can have more time to look at student work. The Friends recognize that their focus on student work generates serious conversation about teaching and improves what they are doing in the classroom.

To allow Ann to be better prepared for her turn, veteran teachers in the CFG agree to present their student work first. When it comes time for Ann to present, she speaks quietly.

> "I have been trying to make group work succeed in my classroom. But it seems that by halfway through the period, my students become restless and unfocused. By the end of class, they have not accomplished much—and certainly have not learned what I hoped that they would. You can see from the examples of work I've passed out that it could be much better. Do you have any ideas to help make my groups function better?"
>
> Then, as the protocol dictates, Ann sits back and listens to Friends discuss her concern. During the discussion, Mark offers an idea:
>
> "Why doesn't Ann limit the size of her groups into three—make them triads? Then, only one student speaks at a time and the other two listen. They will focus more on the task at hand. And the room will be quieter, so Ann can better listen in to what the groups are saying."
>
> When it comes time to debrief, Ann says, "Thank you for your thoughts. I am especially excited about Mark's idea to put my students into triads. I can't wait to try this."

Because Mark Harris participates in the CFG, the notion of a dog-and-pony-show evaluative process between him and Ann becomes moot. Mark, who is relaxed and unassuming, understands the importance of forming a respectful relationship with Ann. He spends time in her classroom, observes her teaching practice, and helps her improve.

He becomes a *de facto* second mentor. Ann feels free to be open about her goals and accepts advice from him. Among his many helpful observations, she learns to move about the room when talking and occasionally lower her voice to a whisper when she needs her students' attention.

~ ~ ~

Shirley and Ann's willingness to open their mentor-protégé relationship to the wider school community made collegiality possible among the staff. As members of their CFG, they now understand that

- all teachers need support and feedback;
- supervisors can look for teachers' potential and participate in their nourishment; and
- to "go public" with one's teaching becomes an important practice.

As a result, the isolated classroom becomes an anomaly—for the protégé, for the mentor, for members of the CFG, and, hopefully, throughout the school. This process breaks the cycle of teachers having to be alone. New teachers will understand from their first days that teaching is a collaborative process where collegiality is the foundation of successful teaching. In this new paradigm, the odds are that fewer new teachers will drop out, whereas now nearly 50 percent leave the profession in their first five years.

POINTS TO PURSUE

Confidentiality

Confidentiality in schools needs thoughtful consideration. Unlike the doctor-patient relationship, much of the work of schools is public. Assessment tests are designed to make public what students have learned or not learned. Teachers and administrators openly discuss students' strengths and weakness, their behaviors, and their potential, particularly when making placements.

Schools need to decide, then, what information is public and what is not. Is your school clear on this matter? If not, what can you do to make it clear?

Classrooms as Private Worlds

For generations of teachers, the classroom has been a private world. A teacher's classroom is often seen as belonging to that teacher. Yet schools are public institutions funded by public funds. The mentor-protégé relationship as described in this chapter opens up classrooms, first to one another and later to colleagues throughout the school.

If you happen to be in a mentor-protégé relationship, discover how the ideas offered in this chapter can enrich it. If your school does not have a mentor program, discuss the need for one with your principal.

Critical Friends

Explore the concept of Critical Friends Groups (CFGs) discussed in this chapter for your school and invite colleagues to form one. When you can examine student work inside a protocol format, you will focus on what matters in teaching, not on your fellow teachers and yourself. As a member of a CFG, you come to know yourself and your colleagues better—and you discover new ideas to improve your teaching.

National School Reform Faculty (Home of Critical Friends)

Visit the National School Reform Faculty's website for rich resources on Critical Friends, particularly protocols and videos. Purchase a copy of the DVD, discussed in this chapter, "Looking at Student Work: A Window into the Classroom" and use it to generate interest in CFGs. See http://www.nsrfharmony.org.

Establish a dialogue with other teachers with your ideas. Log on to Teachingthatmatters.wordpress.com and join the conversation.

NOTES

1. *Teachers* (United Artists, 1984).
2. Paula Evans and Gene Thompson-Grove, "Looking at Student Work: A Window into the Classroom," Annenberg Institute for School Reform, 1997. Also explore the National School Reform Faculty's website, http://www.nsrfharmony.org/, for rich resources on this concept.

TWO
Dialogue: Build Teacher-Administrator Relationships

When teachers welcome administrators to work alongside them, both parties gain valuable feedback essential to an atmosphere that nourishes positive change.

Why don't teachers want to be observed? What holds them back from seeking feedback, especially from administrators? Why are administrators reluctant to visit classrooms? Why do both seem to prefer scheduled dog-and-pony-show evaluations that assure that they will be seen at their best?

Pam Peters leads another mentor workshop, this time with a selected group of twelve seasoned teachers from a well-respected suburban high school. Near the beginning of the first session, Pam comments:

> "Here's an interesting proposition: Once you develop a good relationship with your protégé that allows you to come into their rooms unannounced, you might consider granting the same privilege for your supervisor to visit you unannounced."
>
> For a brief moment, everyone around the table becomes dead quiet. Then Marie Orson, a lively, feisty, and outspoken longtime high school language arts teacher speaks up. "I don't want anyone to be in my room unless I am ready for them."

No one disputes her. No one. Somewhat surprised by this reaction, Pam decides to tell them about Benjamin Zander, a music professor, who faced a similar situation, in his case with his conservatory students. As their teacher, Zander became frustrated because they only wanted to play perfectly for him in order to get their A. They wanted, in effect, to do dog-and-pony shows. He, on the other hand, wanted to break down this grade barrier and be free to become their teacher.

He decided to ask each of them to write a letter in the past tense dated at the end of the term to explain to him how they earned their A. Once they passed in their letter, they no longer had to worry about their grade. They could practice in front of him for real—and he could provide feedback as their teacher. And, if he ever saw one of them not acting as an A student, he could remind him of his commitment.[1]

Pam then suggest that Zander's insight relates to teachers. The choice of teachers to remain in isolated rooms and perform yearly dog-and-pony shows in front of supervisors perpetuates the status quo. Unless teachers find ways to receive real feedback, they will likely not improve.

In the evening after the workshop Marie decides to discuss the Zander letter idea with her husband. As a result, she decides to take a risk and write a Zander-style letter to her supervisor, George Markus, that evening. In her letter she concludes,

> As you can see from the expectations that I've placed on myself, I want you to know me as an accomplished teacher. You can see that I have very high standards for what I want my students to learn by the end of the year. I realize, however, that I need help in taking them there. Teaching has always been difficult, even after having done it for many years. I hope that you will be willing to take time to come into my room and work with me and my students. I know that I try my best on my own, but I might do better if you help me.
>
> You have always been willing to listen when we come to you with problems. At faculty meetings you offer good ideas. And your experience as a teacher gives you a good perspective on what we do every day. I hope that you will decide to help me.
> Sincerely,
> Marie

Marie's act of writing her letter to George opens a dialogue. When they meet, George expresses his surprise.

> "Wow, Marie, I am impressed with your forthrightness. I know that you have a good handle on what you want to accomplish with your students. Do you really mean that you want *me* to come into your room at any time? You want *me* to comment on your teaching?"
>
> "Yes," Marie says, "I realize that I need feedback. You know that I spend much of my time providing feedback to my students while they are learning—what we teachers call *formative* assessment. You know, too, that I ask them to step up to the plate on a test or paper that gives them opportunities to demonstrate what they know, understand, and are able to do—what we all know as *summative* assessment.
>
> "I realize now that I need support with what I am trying to accomplish and direct feedback when I take my turn to step up to the plate."

Now when George enters her room, she hardly pays attention, as she knows why he's there. During one visit, George moves about the room along with Marie assisting different groups. He notices that some of her students struggle with her group-work assignment. Later in the day, Marie asks him for his observations to improve the process. He suggests:

> "Why not vary the size of your groups to fit the social preferences of your students: Keep larger groups (four to five) for the more sociable students and smaller (two to three) for the quieter ones—and allow those who wish to, to reflect on their own.[2] If you try these approaches, let me know if my suggestions help."

Marie and George's interactive relationship establishes a dialogue that builds collegiality. In the traditional scheduled dog-and-pony-show model, the supervisor is not seen as being a part of a partnership. Instead, he appears as an outsider whose main purpose is to judge.

Why then, at the mentor workshop, did Marie resist Pam Peters's suggestion that supervisors observe her "teaching for real?" Why did she indicate that she preferred to hole up inside the protective cocoon of her classroom? Perhaps, at the time she may be have been feeling the threat that administrators have had over teachers for generations. Yet all teachers, including veterans like Marie, require feedback.

After reflecting on and discussing the issue with her husband, Marie changed her mind and wrote a Zander-style letter to George Markus. After welcoming George into her classroom, Marie wonders if her veteran colleagues can also let go of that restrictive mindset. How can they become open to seek help to meet the challenging realities that face them? Surely they recognize that they do not succeed with every student every day. They have too many obstacles to overcome.

Still, many of her colleagues continue to choose to stay inside their isolated classrooms and attempt to meet these challenges alone. They prefer not to ask for help, as they fear they may lose their reputation if seen struggling with students—and, they may not feel safe to ask.

Until teachers and supervisors decide to let go of this restrictive paradigm and, like Marie Orson and George Markus, build a dialogue, they will likely remain mired in past practices. They will not become open to assess what works or not, to take whatever actions are necessary, and to seek support to improve instruction. The example of Marie's decision to write a letter to appeal for help is one way to establish trust and respect between teacher and administration—a dialogue that benefits both parties.

Tradition, on the other hand, has kept both teachers and administrators holding onto their roles where no boats are rocked and classroom practice continues as it always has. Unless this pattern is broken, administrators will not have opportunities to impact the instructional process, nor will teachers come to understand the potential value of administrators in their classrooms.

As difficult as it may be to make happen, when teachers invoke the courage to see each other as peers, they let go of the dog-and-pony-show mindset that prevents both from receiving effective feedback. They make honest dialogue possible in support of teaching that benefits students.

POINTS TO PURSUE

Dog-and-Pony-Shows

These have long been the bane of classroom teaching. As long as evaluations are scheduled, teachers present what they want administrators to see and administrators hope to see that all is well. Thus, everything stays the same.

If you are in a school with this outmoded system, have the courage to follow the lead of Marie Orson in this chapter. She decided to step out of this paradigm and seek feedback from an administrator. Are you willing to take similar steps?

Letter to an Administrator

Benjamin Zander's end-of-the-term letter that he asks his music students to write to him invites teachers to write their own. If you decide to write such a letter, choose to share it with a colleague—or better yet, with an administrator. You will then open channels of communication. Do you have the courage to take such a step?

Letter to My Teacher

Consider using Zander's letter format with your students. Invite them to look ahead for a month (or a week if you think it would work better) and have them write a letter to you dated at the end of the month (or week) about how they earned their A or B or C depending upon the student.

Tell them that visualizing success will help them realize it. Make sure they understand that if they do not fulfill their goals, you'll still have something from which to build. See if this approach improves motivation and behavior.

Open classroom doors

The choice to become open with colleagues—and with supervisors—remains a challenge. The embedded habit of closed-door classrooms reaches back generations. Each time, however, you open your door to others you increase opportunities to find wisdom both from what you share and from what others can offer to you. Try this idea and see what transpires.

Open office doors

Administrators, like teachers, often hunker down behind closed doors, as they have multiple tasks to complete during the day. As a principal or assistant, you can, however, make it a point to open your door and encourage teachers to come in. Opening the door itself may be as important as what happens once teachers come in.

Let go of the fear of being watched

As a supervisor, what steps do you take to become more welcome in classrooms? As a teacher, what will it take to invite administrators and fellow teachers into your room? What steps can you take to relieve the fear of being observed when "teaching for real," when you do not expect anyone to be there? What can you do to initiate a more open process between yourself, your colleagues, and your supervisors?

Establish a dialogue with other teachers with your ideas. Log on to Teachingthatmatters.wordpress.com and join the conversation.

NOTES

1. Ben Zander and Rosamund Zander, *The Art of Possibility: Transforming Professional and Personal Life* (New York: Harvard Business School Press, 2000), chapter 3, "Giving an A," 25–53.

2. Susan Cain, *Quiet: The Power of Introverts in a World That Can't Stop Talking* (New York: Random House, 2013), 255–56. Cain is adamant about making school work for introverts (one-third to one-half of students) who need to be respected with less social interaction and more quiet times.

THREE
Coaching: Provide Nonjudgmental Teacher Support

Active feedback from coaches breaks open the perpetual isolation of the classroom and provides teachers with needed support and new ideas.

Ann Norton keeps her voice at a fever pitch. The closer she comes to making a point, the louder she becomes. By the end of the class, her shrill speech resonates at its highest peak. Tall and well dressed, she is positive, friendly, competent, open, energetic, supportive, caring—and loud.

Pat Carlton, principal of a new charter school, hires a staff in which almost half have three or fewer years experience. She decides to hire Phil Rodgers, an experienced consultant known for his empathy for beginning teachers.

In his first year at the school, he leads a dozen afterschool workshops tailored to the school's needs. The next year, in addition to the workshops, Pat decides that Phil should visit the classrooms of her newest teachers. She wants him to observe each of them for a class period and offer insights to improve their practice. Phil is delighted, as he prefers to act as a coach to observe and help teachers directly. He knows that these teachers, like most, spend nearly all their time alone with students. And they are far too busy to take time to observe one another.

When he sits down with Ann after observing her, he has no difficulty opening the conversation:

"Ann, what do you think about today's lesson?"

"I think it was pretty typical of what I do each day. I make every effort to keep each student focused on the task at hand. You know, the school expects us to keep up with the schedule that we are given each week. I do everything I can to stay on pace. What do you think?"

"For a first-year teacher," Phil replies, "you have remarkable command of your subject matter. Both your introduction to fractions and the paragraph-writing segments were well structured. You obviously knew where you were headed. You seem to know your students well, as you responded effectively to each of them. As for Juan, who you intimated has been difficult recently, you managed to keep him engaged; he never acted out as you said he has in the past.

"And I noticed that you prefer to stand up front for nearly all the period. You keep everyone's attention and use Popsicle sticks to assure that each student has an opportunity to participate."

Then comes the hard part for Phil. He hesitates to bring up the issue of her voice, as he feels that she may take it personally. He wants her to know that he's there as a coach to help her, not evaluate her. He broaches the subject cautiously but directly.

"Ann, have you noticed during the period that your voice becomes louder?"

"I never thought about that. Does it really?"

"Yes, you become very loud. My concern is that if you stay at a high pitch you could not only damage your vocal chords, but you may also offend your students' ears. In fact, you will be better able to keep the attention of your students when you lower your voice, something I learned from a colleague early on in my teaching. Some teachers even suggest that if you whisper, students will have to strain to hear you. I am not suggesting necessarily to whisper, but I am saying that lowering your voice will work better for you and for your students."

"Come to think of it, my throat feels very tired at the end of the day. I will give your suggestion a try. Thank you."

"You're welcome."

A month later Phil returns to the school for a workshop with Ann and her colleagues. Without asking Ann to comment, she allows that she has been using a quieter voice. "It took several days for my students to get used to my new voice," she says, "but now they have!"

Ann made a breakthrough, not only about an aspect of her teaching but also about her power to change her practice. Without feedback, she might not have become conscious of her rising voice level until, perhaps, her throat had started to suffer. She discovered that she could modulate it and at the same time create a positive effect on her students—and on herself. She realized, too, how much better her throat felt at the end of the day.

At that same workshop, Phil expands on Ann's story:

"Once you realize that *you* are the one who decides how you teach, you do not have to teach as you currently do or as you think you're supposed to. Instead, you can pay attention to what works and what does not and feel free to change. And, if you invite colleagues and administrators to observe and share with you what they notice, all the better.

You may have bad habits waiting to be discovered and changed much to the relief of your students—and to you!"

~ ~ ~

Teachers, after all, work in a vacuum. Often, the only feedback they receive comes when supervisors evaluate them. They would be fortunate, however, to have a mentor, a coach, or a colleague who observes them "teaching for real." They could begin on their own by invoking Exit Cards, Recap Cards, and Tickets to Leave to get direct responses from students. And if their school has them, they could use classroom response systems (Clickers) that provide information about what students know and understand during a lesson—and assure anonymity at the same time.[1]

When teachers feel ready, they can ask colleagues to observe them. Once they become familiar with having other people in their classrooms, they might feel comfortable to form a Critical Friends Group as a means to collaborate further with colleagues.[2]

Teachers can invoke steps to break out of the often self-imposed tyranny of the isolated classroom. It's not important which particular devices they use to get feedback from students; they should experiment to see which ones work best. It is important, however, to find colleagues and administrators who can help them see their teaching more clearly and to make it better. And, if they are fortunate, they'll have a nonpartisan coach to nurture their growth.

POINTS TO PURSUE

Offer positive feedback to teachers

Because teachers are sensitive about the quality of their practice, asking for feedback may be risky. Observers need to respect what teachers want. Teachers may see feedback as criticism from observers who share unexpected data or give offhand comments. As an evaluator, you need to set a tone of respect and support. Otherwise, you'll be ineffective.

Gain permission when offering feedback

As a supervisor or coach, when you notice a problem that a teacher may be having but is not aware of it (as happened with Ann's voice in this chapter), build slowly toward bringing it up. Use active listening. Remember, building a relationship is the most important role you have as a supervisor or coach.

Seek anonymous feedback from students (1) Exit Cards

Exit Cards are one way to receive immediate feedback; At the end of a lesson, a unit, or at any time, pass out index cards. Ask students questions in pairs, such as: "I like . . . , I wish . . ."; "Today's big idea for me . . . ," What questions do I have?"; "I want . . . , I need. . . ."

Have them fill them out before leaving class, usually anonymously.[3] You learn about the value of your lesson and students have closure. For multiple classes, use color coded cards, one color for each class.

Seek anonymous feedback from students (2) Recap Cards

Recap Cards are specific, take more time, and provide more information. Unlike "Thumbs Up, Thumbs Down" or asking "How many of you think you know . . . ?" Invoking Recap Cards gives time for students to practice the day's lesson—and receive immediate feedback.

For a detailed description and account of the success of this approach see John Quinn, Brian Kavanagh, Norma Boakes, and Ronald Caro, "Two Thumbs Way, Way Up: Index Card Recap and Review." *Teaching Children Mathematics*, December 2008/January 2009. The National Council of Teachers of Mathematics, 295–303.[4]

Seek anonymous feedback from students (3) Clickers

Clickers are one of the most effective student feedback devices, which have been developed by iClicker at www1.iclicker.com. These devices, either using the iClicker remote or web-based polling tool, can collect data during class from each student anonymously.

In addition, Clickers store each student's responses that can be displayed or not. It's a powerful learning-centered tool and invaluable for seeing where students are at the moment. Immediate assessment!

Seek coaching

Teachers are fortunate when they can work with professional coaches. Coaches are essential to professionals, including singers, athletes, dancers—and teachers.[5] Unfortunately, few teachers have, or choose to have, opportunities to be coached. Coaching can effect change more than professional development workshops. Choosing a competent coach is choosing to get better. How can you make this happen?

Establish a dialogue with other teachers with your ideas. Log on to Teachingthatmatters.wordpress.com and join the conversation.

NOTES

1. See http://en.wikipedia.org/wiki/Classroom_Performance_Systems for an explanation.
2. See chapter 1, "Confidentiality: End Classroom Isolation".
3. At a workshop in October 2000, Grant Wiggins told about a teacher who used Exit Cards with his students every Friday. Since then, I have learned from fellow consultants about various ways to use them. A valuable tool.
4. Thanks to Ginny Tang who led me to this source.
5. See Atul Gawande, "Personal Best" in *The New Yorker*, October 3, 2011, for an insightful look at the role of coaching for all professionals, especially for teachers and doctors.

FOUR

Lessons: Create Ambiguity to Stimulate Thinking

When teachers create open-ended lessons, they allow surprises to emerge both for student and for them.

Tom Mahoney still sees in his mind Ernie, short and gruff, at his seventh-grade desk, the second seat in the middle row. Ernie hates school and scowls at his student teacher. He makes erratic inane comments. He's been irreverent before, but today he gives one of his finest performances. In front of Tom's supervisor, Professor Herbst, who already has expressed his distaste for Tom in his graduate history seminar. Tom's student-teacher grade suffers.

"Ernie, please turn around and face the front. Sam can take care of himself. Now would everyone take out their homework. I want to hear what you decided about...."

"Ernie! Stop slouching and take out your homework! Oh, you didn't do it? Then, please sit quietly."

The class has seen this exchange many times. No one seems moved by Ernie, nor does anyone show their disdain for his behavior. He seems to have power over most of his classmates, perhaps because he is older, as he'd been held back in second and fourth grade. Ernie was one of those kids like Allen Johnson in Tom's childhood who, despite his short stature, intimidated the hell out of him. Tom feels Allen Johnson's presence in Ernie, hence he hesitates to confront him.

"As I was saying, class, what do you know about the ziggurats in Mesopotamia? Why do you think they were built? Jocelyn?"

"Well Mr. Mahoney, I think that men built them to control others. I think, too ..."

"Ernie, what are you doing now? Please go back to your seat. We are discussing our homework!"

And so it went that day. Each time Tom regrouped the class, Ernie found something else to do to interrupt. Tom made it through the lesson, but by the end of the period (it seemed so long!) he was sweating, embarrassed, and upset. He doubts anyone learned much. He was sure that he had a well-designed lesson plan that his social studies methods instructor, Mr. Martz, had taught him how to do. The plan was closely connected to the good work his students did the day before when Ernie was absent, which happened quite often. Unfortunately, not today.

Tom wanted to perform a dog-and-pony show, to create the perfect lesson for Professor Herbst. He knew that if his students were willing to cooperate, all would go well. If they didn't, as Ernie made certain on that day, the lesson quickly deteriorated.

How foolish of Tom, or any teacher, to think that he has to develop the perfect lesson from start to finish, including one for a supervisor. Of course, a teacher needs to take care to design what he intends his students to learn. To do less would be irresponsible. But to imagine that preparation in advance will transfer directly to students misses a great truth about teaching, one that Tom later realized: The moment intentions come into contact with students, most likely they will come undone. Ernie showed him this, but he did not learn it then.

When a teacher insists on students' compliance, he risks shutting down their minds. Musad Amur, a second-year European history teacher—vibrant, confident, and smart—is enamored with his lecture-style teaching. Every day, he stands behind his podium and sets the tone for his students to listen to him and take notes. Most of the time his unkempt hair, animated gestures, and whiteboard diagrams and scribbles with colored markers keep their attention.

When it comes to tests, however, Musad is often surprised at the mixed results. Most of his students pass, but only a few earn A's and a few get D's. Usually his grades replicate the traditional bell curve. Because he feels pressure to keep pace with the curriculum, however, he proceeds directly on to the next unit.

Because he views his students' brains more as receptacles than processors, he chooses only to lecture. He believes that the lecture is the most efficient way to give students knowledge. His one-way style meets the needs of a few but leaves others in the dark.

One day during his planning period, Musad happens to observe a colleague who uses a variety of approaches to engage her students. He notices that they are active, ask questions, and seem more eager to learn than his students. He begins to realize that his strict lecture approach may focus more on what he has to *say* than what his students *need* from him.

At a social studies conference a couple of weeks later, he learns about Mary Budd Rowe's 10-2 method. He sees it as a means for him to continue to lecture but provide students time to process in class. Over the weekend, he organizes his next week's lecture notes into Rowe's format: he intends to intersperse his three ten-minute mini-lectures with two-minute processing times. "A different way to lecture," he says to himself, "but certainly worth a try."

Because Musad is nervous and concerned that his classes might act up about his using 10-2, he decides to try only with his first-period class, as he thinks they might be the most receptive. After several days, however, he senses that his students are not catching on, particularly with the processing times, as many of them socialize with their friends. So he decides that he needs to make his mini-lectures more engaging and provide more structure for the two-minute segments.

After his opening with his mini-lecture about the coming of the French Revolution of 1789, Musad stops to speak with the class:

> "Okay, I hope I've showed you the effect that Marie Antoinette had on the French people. In the next two minutes I want you to make a diagram that shows her relationship with them. Stick figures are fine. I want you to show me visually what you just heard."
>
> Students start to fuss. He insists that they give this idea a try. After much cajoling, they start to settle down. He then resumes with his second mini-lecture on Marie Antoinette. After ten minutes, he stops and says, "Now, I want you to imagine that you are Marie Antoinette. Based on these first two mini-lectures, take two minutes to write a journal entry about the French people from her point of view."
>
> Because his students are used to writing, the class settles quickly. Curious about their intense concentration, he asks a few of them to share their thoughts. One of them even shares her diagram from the previous processing. He then proceeds to his third mini-lecture. He looks at the clock and sees that he's well behind completing his lesson plan.

By the end of the week, Musad realizes that he is not covering as much with his first period class as he had hoped. Yet his students are starting to make good use of the two-minute processing times, particularly when they interact with each other in small groups. He begins to worry that this class is falling behind his other classes—and it is more worrisome that he is falling behind his colleagues.

His neighbor, John Kyle, is already on Robespierre, while Musad is still on the fall of the Bastille. Soon Musad will be meeting with his department, where everyone decides which topics and pages in the textbook they will cover for the next week. He doesn't particularly like this pacing system, as he is beginning to understand that teaching is a series of personal decisions between him and his students.

Still, he finds that his 10-2 students are becoming more involved. More of them complete their assignments. Some are creative with their homework. More seem to enjoy class. They earn better grades on quizzes and tests. And they leave class with more smiles, as they sense that they have learned something in class, rather than having to take notes to study at home.

Soon these students become more open to the interplay between his mini-lectures and the two-minute segments. He begins to include their thinking as to the structure of the lectures and segments. Together, they form a flexible process that moves the class in intriguing directions. In creating results together, everyone learns. After a month, Musad says to his first-period group:

> "I am impressed with the amount of work that you are doing. While you know that I love to lecture, I really like the way that I've been doing it with you. You may have noticed that I do not always stay within the ten minutes that I said I would; sometimes I go shorter and occasionally I talk longer—and sometimes I allow more time for you to process.
>
> "However, at the beginning of my new approach you struggled with the two-minute processing times. For those of you who excelled with my regular lecture-and-test-taking format, you've found it particularly hard to readjust. As for me, I struggle to come up with ways for you to use the processing times productively. Do any of you have ideas about how we might better use them?"
>
> After a pause, Marty Rosen raises his hand. "I wonder if you could let us form groups of two or three before you start your mini-lectures. I think we'd learn more."
>
> "I think that's a good idea, Marty. I will try that. Michele?"
>
> "I agree with Marty. And, I think you should let us decide how we process on what you tell us."
>
> "That's good, Michele. I'll try that. I also have a couple more ideas. First, during long blocks, particularly if we use Marty's idea of groups of only two or three, I will ask groups to combine and compare notes. Then, I will ask some to report their conclusions to the class.
>
> "Second, I will provide more opportunities for each of you to process on your own. I know for some of you this quiet time will be a welcome respite from the social pressures of the regular classroom. Many of you prefer quiet times for reflection. For those of you who think that you might not like reflecting on your own, you will have an opportunity to discover just how good this can be for you. I trust that you will give it your best shot."

In the past month, Musad has made a remarkable transition. He's moved away from thinking that he must complete specific outcomes without considering his students' needs. He now understands that he can design lessons that are open to ambiguity, open to surprise. He sees that a successful perfect lesson relies on its imperfection, on its flaws that invite reconsideration, and on its lack of precision that encourages insights.

Musad now recognizes that teaching is an uncertain profession. Uncertainty invites teacher and students together to engage in evolving the class. The best times occur "in-the-moment." Sometimes, as Musad discovers, they are so intense that immediately afterwards he cannot recall exactly what just happened.

He treasures those lessons when time flies by, especially during long blocks when his plans leave open possibilities. He has a clear idea of where his class is headed for the week, for the unit, for the term, and for the year. Yet he remains open as to how to get there—and welcomes surprise landings when they occur. He relies on his students as they proceed down "the road less traveled," "to the promised land." He trusts their questions, insights, and ideas—and his own as well.

Musad knows that in today's culture, with its myriad electronic distractions, students will have been in many places in the twenty-four hours or weekend between classes. He has noticed that his first-period class in which he uses 10-2 thinking connects with previous lessons better than his other classes. He realizes that these engaged lessons invite ambiguity, raise questions, allow for insights—and improve retention.

When teachers become obsessed with covering material to meet others' strict expectations, as Musad used to do, they forget to focus on what students are actually learning. Young teachers are particularly vulnerable when they notice students trying to push a lesson in a different direction. The more they struggle to stay with their intentions—as Tom Mahoney tried with Ernie in front of his supervisor—the more they might think they are failing. Some may begin to feel that they are not good teachers. They feel guilty about their performance and fear judgment from others. It's tough teaching alone.

One important lesson for young teachers as they proceed down unanticipated paths is to include student input, as Musad does. Of course, teachers need to discern when not to trust student diversions. When they know their content well, like Musad, they can recognize that an unforeseen path might be heading either toward a dead end *or* toward new possibilities, and hence they can relax and go with the energy of the class. They discover that the wisdom of collective brains exceeds the sum of individuals.

POINTS TO PURSUE

When planning, anticipate the unexpected

When planning lessons, you need to anticipate possible shifts. When you take time to anticipate you will be better prepared when the lesson takes a sudden turn. At least, you will not be surprised. What can you do to prepare for the unexpected?

Lectures and grades

Did you notice what Musad Amur discovered about his choice to solely lecture to students: that their test grades usually replicated a bell curve? Have you thought of varying your teaching as Musad has, so as to increase chances of success for more students? What might you do?

The 10-2 thinking alternative

Musad Amur chooses to try 10-2 thinking, as he hopes to make his lectures more palatable, more connective, more engaging. His decision to begin with only one class allows him to compare results with his regular classes. He struggles when he feels he is falling behind. His persistence with implementing 10-2 thinking, however, pays off.

Take a close look at the effects of your teaching on student success. If students are struggling, don't blame them. Have the courage to seek different approaches, such as 10-2 or the many others suggested in this book.

Pacing

The expectation that teachers in a department need to be on the same page every day (or at least for the week) deserves careful scrutiny. Pacing implies that coverage is more important than what students actually learn. It means the textbook drives lessons. And it deprives teachers and students of pursuing unforeseen paths that could be more meaningful.

If you are in this predicament, see what you can do to free yourself from this straitjacket.

Knowing your content allows for student participation

The more familiar you are with the content of your teaching, the more flexible you can be. To know content well allows you to be open to student queries and can make your teaching richer and more fun for everyone. You can make room for student input and then have a choice to go with it or not. What do you think of this attitude?

One the other hand, if you plan to teach, or are asked to teach, a subject new to you, be open to learning it with your students. Don't pretend to know. Let learning together become an adventure for everyone. Not knowing can lead to knowing.

Invoke ambiguity

To decide to make ambiguity central to teaching is doubly difficult. First, it may take time away from completing expected coverage of material. Second, many students do not like gray areas. They want to know what to do and then be able to get it done quickly.

Are you willing to take time to be open to ambiguity and to teach your students its value? It will take time. Necessary time.

Establish a dialogue with other teachers with your ideas. Log on to Teachingthatmatters.wordpress.com and join the conversation.

FIVE

Conversation: Make Time for Reflective Talking and Listening

When teachers hold face-to-face conversations, their classrooms have a sense of purpose, thoughtfulness, and adventure.

Conversations are building blocks for learning. They allow collective wisdom to emerge. Margaret Wheatley provides a unique set of six principles for valuing conversations. Her poetic and insightful book, *Turning to One Another: Simple Conversations to Restore Hope to the Future*,[1] invites teachers to put listening at the center of their classrooms. Her frontispiece quotes Rainer Maria Rilke:

> You must give birth to your images.
> They are the future waiting to be born.
> Fear not the strangeness you feel.
> The future must enter you long before it happens.
> Just wait for the birth, for the new hour of clarity.

What is Rilke saying? What does he mean by "the future must enter you long before it happens"? And what in that future will touch our lives? Whenever we meet people, some we accept, others we pass by. Why we choose to connect with one person and not another remains a mystery.[2]

Wheatley describes her conversation process:

> For conversation to take us into this deeper realm [being part of a greater whole to discover our collective wisdom] I believe we have to practice several new behaviors. Here are the principles I've learned to emphasize before we begin a formal conversation process.
> We acknowledge one another as equals.
> We try to stay curious about each other.

We recognize that we need each other's help to become better listeners.
We slow down so we have time to think and reflect.
We remember that conversation is the natural way we humans think together.
We expect it to be messy at times.[3]

What are the implications of Wheatley's six principles for the classroom?

We acknowledge one another as equals.

Marta McGuinness, a perky brunette with her signature ponytail, has been a middle school language arts teacher for five years. She brings her vibrant self to school every day. Her seventh-grade students look forward to her lessons, as they often do not know what to expect. At the same time, they know that she has high expectations for them.

Recently, Marta discovered Margaret Wheatley's six principles for valuing conversations. She already holds frequent discussions. Last year, she discovered Edward DeBono's *Six Hat Thinking* and incorporated his "Six Hats" into some of her discussions. She likes the traditional link between "thinking" and "hats," the ease of switching hats, and the role that each hat defines. She finds that by giving students Six-Hat roles, their discussions become more focused.

Each hat specifies a direction and focus for thinking. Wearing a hat, students learn the value of different perspectives that contribute to a better understanding of an issue. For students who are prone to talk, having to wear a particular hat makes them pause before speaking. And for those who tend not to participate but might want to, having a particular hat provides them an opening.[4]

Wheatley's first principle, *We acknowledge one another as equals*, hits home, as it brings attention to an idea that Marta had not considered: She needs to let go of making prejudgments about her students' capabilities. This principle encourages her to be less the teacher who knows best and more the teacher who looks for what's best in her students. She decides to make this paradigm one of her mantras.

As equals in the classroom, Marta realizes that the teacher and students can build trust that allows for authenticity, honesty, and risk. No one sits in fear of giving a wrong answer or asking a stupid question. Minds are free to explore their own or other's ideas. Everyone becomes peers in pursuit of questions, perplexities, and understandings. They may or may not reach their goal, but when they do, they are often surprised. They may even arrive at unexpected destinations. Marta realizes that it's all good.

Her longtime habit of putting chairs in a circle for discussions has helped her students acknowledge themselves as equals. By not having to look at the backs of the heads of their peers they relate more directly with one another.

We try to stay curious about each other.

Sometimes we need only to be present. Marta discovers this at one of her weekly group meditations. After sitting practice, she moves onto the floor beside Brenda Morton whom she's not seen for several months. Because Brenda has been seriously ill, Marta wants to know how she is feeling now.

"How are you?"

For the next ten minutes Marta simply listens. She does not speak. She pays attention. Each feels the presence of the other, Marta curious about Brenda's health and Brenda curious about Marta's attentiveness. Before they stand up, they decide to stay in touch.

The next day, Marta attempts to carry the epiphany of that attentiveness into her classroom. She wants to be as open to her students as she was to Brenda. She knows that in class she cannot listen one-on-one, yet she still makes an effort to direct her curiosity toward each of them. She wishes she could be better, but she persists.

When we care to be attentive, as happened with Brenda and Marta, we listen.

We recognize that we need each other's help to become better listeners.

Because our minds are attuned to interruptions, listening deeply becomes difficult. If we intend, for example, to pay full attention while writing on the computer, we hide incoming mail-alert notifications. At dinner we choose to ignore the telephone. When with friends, we pause, turn off our iPhones, and listen attentively to their stories that always remind us of our humanness.

Yet, we live in a fast-paced culture in which information has become more bits, fewer bytes—and certainly fewer sentences. We feel pressure to keep pace with multiple alerts. As we do, we find ourselves swimming inside endless loops; we fear that if we don't respond we'll be left out. It's no wonder students sitting face-to-face in classrooms struggle to communicate, their minds anticipating the next bling.

The more people attend to personal devices, the less time they have face-to-face. They pass one another on the street with heads down engrossed in smartphones. Teachers observe students who are less able to speak to each other face-to-face. Yet teachers yearn to hear from them. They realize that they need to teach them how to converse.

Marta notices that her students have more difficulty engaging in discussion even when sitting in a circle. Instead of lamenting the situation, she decides to teach them how to converse.

> "Well, class, you seem to be having trouble with our discussions. At first, I thought that I have not been asking you good questions, but I realize that you also have trouble speaking directly to one another. So, we are going to do an exercise together. It's called "Inside-Outside Circles."[5]
>
> "Please stand up and push your desks to the side of the room. Now, form two circles. Those of you whose last names begin with *A* to *M*, make an inside circle facing out; those with last names from *N* to *W*, form an outside circle facing in. Be sure that you are facing a classmate." After a few minutes and some redirection, they are ready.
>
> "Now I am going to give you a topic to discuss. I want the person on the inside to speak first for a minute; I'll let you know when the minute's up. Then, the outside person will have a minute to respond to what the inside person said. Then, I'll ring my bell. Other than sticking to the topic, the only requirement is that you look into the other person's eyes as you speak and listen.
>
> "Ready? Okay. Here's my question: 'Now that we are almost through our poetry unit, who is one of your favorite poets *or* what is one of your favorite poems?'"
>
> After both students have their turn to speak, Marta rings the bell. "Okay, now, will the inner circle please move one step to the left to meet a new partner. Again, talk about a favorite poet or poem." After another two minutes, she rings the bell again. "All right, will the inner circle people please move again one step to the left. . . ."

Marta is pleased at how well this exercise flows, except with her third-period class where several students have difficulty looking into each other's eyes. The next day, after some discussion, she convinces the class to try again. The difference this time is that each person speaks for only thirty seconds. Because they do better, she is pleased.

She then decides to do another exercise with all of her classes:

> "Today, as promised, we will discuss Robert Frost's 'The Road Not Taken.' Instead of our usual way of conversing, however, I want you to try a new approach. Before you take a turn to speak, repeat what the previous person has said. Do the best that you can.
>
> "This process will help you to become better listeners. It will certainly slow the conversation, but it will force all of us to pay close attention to what a classmate says. Furthermore, by repeating, you may absorb more of what you heard."
>
> Ivan Milne immediately raises his hand and blurts out, "But, Ms. McGuinness, what if I can't say it exactly?"
>
> "That's all right, Ivan. I want you to try as best as you can. Anytime we are learning something new, we have to be patient with ourselves. Don't worry, Ivan, don't let this idea keep you from participating. You always have interesting things to say."
>
> "All right, Ms. McGuinness."

Once her students successfully learn to repeat what the others say, which took several tries for most classes, she teaches them how to paraphrase. Later she shows them how to mirror and validate what another person says; she hopes these processes will help them develop empathy, something she has noticed is becoming less common among her students.

As for her part in the conversation process, she visualizes a thread that passes through each person who speaks—and, as she observes the flow, she curtails the number of times the thread of the conversation passes through her. She wants students to become involved with each other.

She also decides to build specific listening skills that students can learn to use for oral reports, films, and debates. And for after school, she invites students to join a film/book club in which everyone agrees to turn off their electronic devices.

One evening as she was assessing her efforts to raise the level of conversation with her students, she realizes that at the deepest level of good conversation is inventing. During conversations when she finds herself inventing images, rather than simply communicating information, she discovers that she enjoys them much more. She is not sure, however, if she could communicate this idea to her students.[6]

We slow down so we have time to think and reflect.

Every day, Marta does her best to be open as to what happens in her classroom. She listens to students without forming her own thoughts. She makes every effort to stay in the moment. She resists anxieties about the future and about concerns over which she has no control. No one, she realizes, can make anyone slow down. People have to do it themselves.

Marta also understands that if her students are to develop long-term memories, she needs to provide time for reflection in the classroom. When she pressures her students to keep pace with the flow of information, she sometimes forgets to give them time to consolidate their thoughts.

Nothing stays. They don't remember. When they fail to converse with one another, they live as if they are passing through the night. Without opportunities to spend time in reflection, they may not discover what is deep within them. Taken together, conversations and reflection invite minds to ponder, choose, and retain.

We remember that conversation is the natural way we humans think together.

Throughout human history, the nature of conversations has changed. Early humans developed language by sitting around the campfire telling stories; their memories stored knowledge. The introduction of writing allowed for communication without having to memorize or stay face-to-face. Later, books allowed for connection through uninterrupted solitude, the thoughts of the writer communicating to the reader. Still later, the telephone provided voice-to-voice connections, sightless conversations but conversations nonetheless.

The Internet and wireless devices are taking the world in a new direction, one that often leads to communication without conversation. Social networks dominate. Except for unusual situations, such as the Arab Spring, text messaging and Twitter share tiny bytes of information that tell without serious meaning. People know instantly what they want to know, respond, or pass on—and soon forget what they just read. Like skipping stones.

Does real conversation have a chance in this milieu? Is it still possible for us to commit to face-to-face presence? Do we have the patience? Can we spend time immersed in thought without the need to stay connected? Can the classroom be society's salvation?

Marta seems to thinks so.

We expect it to be messy at times.

When teachers let go of trying to be in control, surprises emerge, insights abound, and joy surfaces. Marta knows that some of her best conversations with students happen when the conversations take on lives of their own. Messiness invites originality. It creates novelty as it pushes everyone away from routine, from predictability.

Marta, like all good teachers, makes plans. Sometimes her students try to subvert them; they move off topic and occasionally succeed until the bell rings. Marta recognizes that despite careful planning, some of her best lessons take exciting detours. Most of the time, she finds a way to stay in the general vicinity of her intentions. Sometimes, however, conversations spawn unforeseen insights never before imagined. Insights from her students. Insights from her.

~ ~ ~

As teachers consider Wheatley's six principles, they can evoke Rilke's words: "You must give birth to your images. / They are the future waiting to be born." Teachers like Marta McGuinness allow conversations to take her and her students to new places. They let go of control and delivery. They allow for the birth of images to appear in their students—and in them.

Because she has found success with Wheatley's six principles, Marta wants to share them with her colleagues. She's discovered that implementing these principles raises questions about what to teach. She asks her principal, Sandra Wang, if she can share these principles at a faculty meeting—and bring up questions derived from them. Sandra agrees.

After passing out Wheatley's six principles and clarifying them, Marta projects her questions:

> 1. In today's rush to meet unified standards and outside assessments, can we still make room for deep conversations?
> 2. What if we fail to teach students how to engage in conversations?
> 3. What if, instead, we only teach them how to take tests?
> 4. What are the consequences if we curtail time for questions in class?
> 5. If we do not choose to engage and listen, how well will students be prepared to live in a future fraught with unpredictability?
> 6. Finally, if we fail to have conversations with our students, will we be ignoring a fundamental quality of human experience? What will be the cost?

"I want to thank Sandra for giving me this opportunity to share these questions. It seems to me that as a faculty we need to discover ways to engage our students on issues that matter. I have found Margaret Wheatley's six principles for valuing conversations that you have before you to be a guide that has enabled me to develop better ways of listening to my students.

"I have also come up with these six questions that I think will help us to pay better attention to the effects of our teaching. Sandra has agreed to allow us to discuss them and see what conclusions we can draw. We've decided to break you up into seven groups as listed on the chart paper behind me. We've purposely mixed you up, rather than keep you in departments. I hope you'll find this approach refreshing.

"If any of you would prefer to think alone or in pairs, please feel free to excuse yourselves from your group. We will take about a half hour before we reconvene for sharing."

The meeting went better than either Marta or Sandra anticipated. Marta thought that she would receive some flack from colleagues, as some might see her as usurping the role of the administration. Surprisingly, several teachers told her afterwards that they liked that she took initiative to engage the faculty. Some began to think about what they might do.

Conversations free up thinking. They allow for a flow of ideas. Yet human culture is evolving in unanticipated directions, which is most noticeable in the behavior of the young. When a group of teenagers sits around a table, often no one seems to be with anyone because each is attending to his smartphone. When they walk together, they frequently text on their phones instead of talking to each other. Digital interconnectivity is king—and it is driving people apart from one another.

Teachers indicate frustration with the obvious distractibility of students as they appear less and less willing to participate. However, if teachers decide to invoke Margaret Wheatley's six principles, as Marta McGuinness has, they can begin to reengage students. Face-to-face conversations will emerge as a natural part of the classroom. It will take patience, much work—and a lot of listening.

Can teachers afford, then, not to have conversations with their students?

POINTS TO PURSUE

Six Hat Thinking

In this chapter Marta McGuinness discovers ways to better engage her middle school students. She discovers Edward De Bono's path-breaking Six-Hat parallel-thinking method that brings structure to her discussions, increases student awareness of the thinking process, and improves participation. First, read Edward De Bono's *Six Thinking Hats* (Little Brown, 1999) for a thoughtful perspective.

Next, explore the web. You can begin with Bart Stewart, http://www.draftymanor.com/bart/sixhats.htm and then to De Bono at http://www.debonogroup.com/six_thinking_hats.php. Check out Images for the Six Hats on Google as well.

See students as they are

When confronted with too many students, teachers find it tempting to sort them out as quickly as they can: Which ones are receptive, which are resistant, which are easy, which are difficult, etc. Margaret Wheatley, however, asks us "to acknowledge each other as equals," therefore not to prejudge.

You must be vigilant to see each student as she is each day—much in the same spirit as Marta was with Brenda at meditation—and not assume that you know what a student will say or do next. A difficult challenge but an effort worth every minute.

Build attention spans through listening skills

How do you see the attention spans of your students? When you see that they are unable to pay attention, are you willing to change what you are doing? Are you willing to take time to discover what will hold them, what will keep them focused?

Reexamine Marta McGuinness's ideas in this chapter and try them yourself. Invoking conversations may open the way to a more engaged classroom, as it has for Marta.

Build retention through reflection

Given the pressure of having to cover material, teachers struggle to find time for students to think and reflect in class. Yet Margaret Wheatley advocates doing just that. She suggests to step back from the need to make haste and recognize the supreme value of taking time for reflection.

After conversations, set aside time for students to reflect—you may well have to teach them how—and see what effect it has on retention. Taken together, conversations and reflection invite minds to ponder, to choose, to retain.

Seek help from colleagues

"The classroom as society's salvation"? Marta has decided to do her best to instill conversation into her classroom. She recognizes the increasing challenge of this goal.

What is your position on this matter? In your school, seek out those teachers who are known for engaged classrooms where students discuss and argue. Ask them to help you learn how you can better involve your students in face-to-face encounters. Don't hesitate.

Engage fellow faculty

Marta discovers an idea that works so well that she wants to share it with her colleagues. Do you have a method, pedagogy, or concept that you'd like to share? Why wait for the administration to decide the agenda for faculty meetings? Propose your idea and see what transpires. Your colleagues may thank you for it.

Establish a dialogue with other teachers with your ideas. Log on to Teachingthatmatters.wordpress.com and join the conversation.

NOTES

1. Margaret Wheatley, *Turning to One Another: Simple Conversations to Restore Hope to the Future* (San Francisco: Berret-Koehler, 2002).
2. My path to Margaret Wheatley's book came from a magazine article that she co-authored with Peter Senge. He is a personal friend and father of one of my former students. Had I seen her article apart from Peter's input to it, I might have passed it by.
3. Margaret Wheatley, *Turning to One Another*, 29.
4. Edward de Bono, *Six Thinking Hats* (MICA Management Resources, 1999). Every teacher would benefit using the Six Hats in their classroom.
5. I learned about this technique from Peg Mongiello.
6. James Hillman wrote, "Inventing images while conversing is certainly more pleasurable than communicating information" in *The Force of Character and the Lasting Life* (New York: Random House, 1999), 171.

SIX

Research: Bring Brain Research Into the Classroom

Teachers who implement proven brain research practices expand learning opportunities for their students.

Teachers sign their initial contract and fully expect to teach throughout their career in much the same way that they were taught. They see it as steady work with little or no likelihood of dismissal. Becoming a teacher requires relatively little preparation and only minimal expectations to maintain certification. Summers off and vacation days with their family are frequently factors in deciding to become a teacher.

But these days are numbered, as the demands on teaching require new thinking. Teachers are feeling pressure to respond to globalization, to the changing cultural landscape—and every day, to their digitally dependent students. If teachers are to meet these challenges, they need to stay open to new research and seek ways to make their classrooms more palatable.

Brain research is one field that teachers have toyed with but for the most part have not taken seriously, perhaps with good reason. For example, the shoddiness of research behind "The Mozart Effect" and "Baby Einstein" has caused people to steer clear of their claims.

But teachers can not allow such shams to serve as an excuse to ignore viable research. Instead, they can seek out well-documented research—and not only brain research—that can assist them to become better teachers in this fast-changing world. To ignore such resources, in some people's eyes at least, could be considered malpractice.

What will entice teachers to adopt a mindset that actively looks for ways to improve their teaching? "Why bother," a teacher might ask, "to push harder than my colleague next door when we both receive the same pay?" The answer is obvious: "I do it for my students and their families—and for myself. I can become an active solicitor of ideas, methods, and practices to improve opportunities for learning. I do not do what I do simply because I've always done it."

No professional field tolerates status quo behavior. People expect doctors and dentists to use the latest instruments, techniques, and medicines. The same principles hold true for lawyers, auto technicians, beauticians, shoe salesmen, restaurateurs, roofers, and cleaning services to name a few. Why are teachers often the exception?

If teachers want to transform their teaching, they can begin by exploring the field of brain research. A good way to begin would be to Google recognized figures in the field, including Eric Jensen, John Medina, David Sousa, and Robert Greenleaf. For example, Eric Jensen, a long-recognized practitioner, has reached thousands of educators through books, conference presentations, and the web. His website provides instant downloads, including his "10 Brain-Based Teaching Strategies," which provide proven principles to incorporate into the classroom.[1]

Searching websites is a good place to begin, but to become deeply engaged in this research, teachers need to spend time in further study. When on a website, people tend to read with less focus; watch someone's eyes reading on the web compared to reading a book. With books and print they are more likely to probe and ponder. Books, whether in paper or e-format, encourage more time for reflection. (This perception may be more true for veteran teachers.)

Begin with a visit to John Medina's lively website, www.brainrules.net, where he introduces the "grump factor" that assures that only peer-review studies support his twelve brain rules. Once you are enticed with his ideas, take the time to read his seminal book, *Brain Rules*.[2] He invites readers to adopt twelve proven brain-researched practices. He writes in layman's language without dumbing down his message. Teachers who choose to incorporate Medina's recommendations will invigorate learning in their classrooms, as demonstrated later in the chapter.

David Sousa has a multiple-book collection on brain research based on his now classic *How the Brain Learns*.[3] In addition to his impeccable research, his "Practitioner's Corner" segments provide teachers useful ways to apply his research in the classroom. And, he writes clearly.

Serious students of brain research will want to read the National Research Council's *How People Learn*.[4] This work remains the definitive compilation of brain-based thinking. Three sections, "Key Findings," "Implications for Teaching," and "Designing Classroom Environments," alone are worth serious study and discussion.[5]

But ultimately, reading is only a beginning. Students will not benefit unless teachers decide to put proven brain-research practices into their classrooms. Implementing two practices from John Medina and one from Eric Jensen described here can make an immediate difference.

MEDINA'S BRAIN RULE #1—EXERCISE (EXERCISE IMPROVES COGNITION.)

How can schools ignore the obvious value of exercise? "Physical activity is cognitive candy," Medina writes.[6] Yet increasing numbers of schools have eliminated recess in order to provide more time for test preparation. Atlanta has constructed schools without playgrounds.[7] Massachusetts does not require physical education; half of its students do not participate in any exercise during the school day.[8]

David Thompson, a dynamic, popular teacher, notices increasing numbers of his middle school math students becoming overweight and lazy. In his search to find new and different ways to engage students, he discovers John Medina's ideas about exercise in his book group. An avid volleyball player, David knows the importance of keeping in shape. He decides that he wants to include physical activities into his lessons. One day after lunch, he tries something new with his seventh graders.

> "Okay class, please stand up. Follow me." A head taller than his tallest student, David starts to jog slowly around his room. Perplexed at first, some start to follow him. "Come on the rest of you, join us!" Soon the whole class is moving around the room. After three minutes, David says, "Okay back to your seats. Now that you know how to do this, every day from now on when you enter the room, put your books on a desk and start jogging just as we have. Any questions?'
>
> "Mr. Thompson, why are you doing this to us?" asks Martin Simpson, a somewhat overweight student. "Are we the only class who has to do this?"
>
> "No Martin, you are the first. All my classes will do it. No doubt you are wondering why I am having you jog around the room. Think of all the hours that you have to sit in classes—and then you have only two ten-minute recesses and only one PE class for the week. Clearly, you—and I—need more exercise. So, that's why I am asking you to jog with me.
>
> "And Martin, from now on, you and your classmates will stand every time you are called on. Once you either answer a question or share an idea, you can turn to your neighbor who will also stand up and do five high-fives together—or you can do them with me. Another opportunity to move about during class."
>
> "I don't think it's fair!" says Maureen Oberman, one of his more outspoken students. "We don't have to in any other classes."
>
> "Fair or not," David says, "it's important that you move about more every day. Besides, I know from my knowledge of recent brain research—I read books, you know!—that activity stimulates the brain,

and an active brain learns more and retains more. You'll see in a month's time when you do better on tests and quizzes.

"One other thing: Before you take a quiz or test, I will put you through some stretching and movement exercises, again to activate your brains. You'll like that, I'm sure. Wait and see."

Just before the bell, David asks his students to pick up their books and stand up. Then, he starts to jog around the room again. "Come on everyone. A couple of last laps with your books in hand before your next class." Most jump up, a few balk, but in the end they all join him. When the bell rings, David opens the door and sends them on their way.

A few students in the hall stop in their tracks wondering what is going on.

David is pleased at how well his new exercise plan works. The next day, he introduces it to all of his other classes. By the end of a month he's tried other ideas to enliven participation, including having students stand up on one foot when speaking, turning round three times when saying "yes" and once when saying "no," and sometimes pantomiming when asking a question. He is pleased that not only do his students cooperate, but also their grades improve. "Thank you John Medina," David says to himself.

JOHN MEDINA'S *BRAIN RULE* #7— SLEEP (SLEEP WELL, THINK WELL.)

Medina makes a cogent argument for the value of good sleep and naps to improve learning. Given the schedules of most schools, high school teachers in particular may wonder what they can do about this rule, as adolescents, according to Medina tend to be "camels" (late to bed, late to get up), rather than "larks" (who are the opposite).[9]

David Thompson's colleague, Paul Ross, teaches ninth grade language arts at the high school. He is in David's book group that has read and discussed Medina's *Brain Rules*. Paul, who is somewhat conservative and formal, is the skeptic of the group. He becomes receptive to new ideas only when he is convinced of their merit. As a "lark," he awakes an hour before school and is eager to begin his first class at 7:30 AM. Because he struggles with his "camel" students, he thinks Medina's ideas on napping may possibly have merit.

"Good morning, chickadees. I see that you are up and at 'em this morning. Hey, Peter, pick your head up off your desk and have a listen. You know how hard it is for you to be in this class at 7:30. No doubt nearly all of you'd rather be in bed. Well, I have an idea that might help you.

"From now on, I want you to come to class *and* put your head on your desk. I will give you ten minutes to take what we'll call a power nap. Either you can do it, or if you're wide awake, you can sit quietly, read, do more homework, or come to talk with me. I bet, however, that most of you will take the nap. Make sense?"

"Come on Mr. Ross, you know that you can't do that!" Andy Knoch blurts out. "What will Principal Norton say? We're not supposed to sleep in class!"

"Well, good point. Don't worry about Principal Norton. I will speak to him in time. Meanwhile, why not get started on your first in class nap. Okay?"

Heads drop one by one and soon the room is silent. After ten minutes, Paul proceeds with his lesson and wonders if they are paying better attention. "The jury's out on this," he says to himself. "I'll have to do this for a while to see if it makes any difference."

In the next couple of weeks, Paul's students enter the room and immediately put their heads down on their desks. His lessons become more lively and students appear to be learning more. For those classes that he teaches later in the morning, he induces power naps whenever he sees students acting logy. These naps, too, seem to help.

Medina also stresses the importance of early afternoon naps when most people's brains are "flatlined" between the "camels" and the "larks." Rest at this time enables the mind to learn better.[10] To test Medina's claim, David Thompson decides to incorporate after-lunch naps for his middle schoolers. Sometimes, he has them jog afterward.

He recognizes, however, that he faces a conundrum: If he doesn't implement naps, he is choosing to ignore the research; if he does, he figures that he will face challenges from administration and colleagues about taking time off task. David intends to tell Paul and other members of their book group of his decision. And perhaps his decision will foster a productive conversation among staff members.

ERIC JENSEN'S TIP SEVEN FROM HIS "10 MOST EFFECTIVE TIPS FOR USING BRAIN BASED TEACHING & LEARNING."

Kathleen Levy teaches sixth-, seventh-, and eighth-grade art in David's school. She received her training at the art department at her local state university. She decided then to become a teacher, as she knew how difficult it would be to make a living as a painter. Besides she had yet to put in her ten thousand hours of deliberate practice that she knows she would have to do to become a competent artist.[11] A member of David and Paul's book group, she decides to share her pent-up frustration about having to teach so many students—and in short class periods.

"I have over four hundred students each week. And I have three preps! Can you imagine such a load for your courses? I'll bet you can't!"

"Right from the first day I was hired, I knew that I was taking on an impossible situation. How can any kid learn art once a week in a forty-five minute class in which at least ten minutes is for set-up and pick-up?

"For two of my classes, I have to use an art cart and wheel it from room to room. Those classes are really impossible to conduct!"

"Wow, Kathleen, I did not realize that your days were like that," said David.

"Neither did I," said Paul.

"Well, I still believe in having art for kids, but I know that it must be done differently. I read "Tip Seven" last week on Eric Jensen's website that advocates more arts education in schools. Jensen draws on the research of neuroscientists—get this—at the University of Oregon, Harvard, the University of Michigan, Dartmouth, and Stanford! Their combined research confirms that—now this will blow you away—the arts boost attention, working memory, and visual-spatial skills, as well as social skills, empathy, timing, patience, verbal memory, and other transferable life skills!"[12] Kathleen repeats this list to make her point.

"My goodness," says Paul, "how can anyone ignore this list? I wonder which of these I teach in my classes?"

"I wonder, too," says David.

"Let me tell you more," Kathleen continues. "The report states that students gain the most value from the arts when they have them from thirty to sixty minutes a day three to five days a week! Not only do my students have art only once a week, but they also only have it for a quarter of the year! At least they get some art," she sighs, "as I know of other schools that have dropped the arts altogether in favor of test preparation."

Kathleen is obviously concerned about the decrease of the arts in schools. She wants colleagues to become advocates of the arts, including integrating them into their subjects. Given the overwhelming evidence in support of arts programs, she hopes to convince school officials to accept nothing less. It's about the students and what they need in order to become well-rounded and healthy human beings. Her book group agrees to do what they can. Yet they understand the difficult challenge of trying to change a school's culture.

David Sousa's concept of "Primacy-Recency" deserves special attention. This concept illustrates how the brain learns during any given learning episode. According to Sousa, the best time to develop long-term retention occurs at the front end of a lesson and the next best time is in the closing minutes; in the down time between, students should be given time to process material. In a forty-five-minute period, for example, a teacher can choose to do one Primacy-Recency lesson *or* to do two twenty-minute Primacy-Recency lessons.[13]

José Gonzalez, another member of the book group, thinks that Sousa's Primacy-Recency would help activate learning in his forty-minute sixth-grade math classes. He decides to try Sousa's sequence with his last-period group.

> Without taking attendance or taking time to collect homework, José asks his students immediately to take out their notebooks. Using his SMART Board, he launches into demonstrating methods for deriving the Pythagorean Theorem, a concept he had briefly touched on before.
>
> After nearly ten minutes of providing input (Sousa's "Primacy"), he tells his students to pair up for the next twenty minutes and develop examples of how the Pythagorean Theorem could work in their lives (Sousa's "down time"). Toward the last ten minutes of the period, he asks each pair to join another pair and summarize the ideas they've discovered (Sousa's "Recency").
>
> Before they leave, José asks them to fill out a ticket-to-leave on a four-by-six card using a process that he's taught them. He asks them to select one idea they liked best and write it on the front and on the back write a question that they'd like for a quiz or test. José collects the cards as his students leave the room.

At first his students are confused with this different sequence, particularly with the processing segment. José decides, however, to stick with his plan, as he is convinced of the validity of Sousa's research. "Why," he asks himself, "should he do most of the work from the front of the room, when his students could be more active during class and, as a result, learn?"

After several weeks, his students grow more accustomed to this approach—and discover that they are retaining more. José sees that Sousa's structure makes for more active and successful learning for his middle schoolers. Having listened to David and Paul speak about their use of naps and physical exercise, he wonders if he should include these brain research ideas with his students as well.

Change is hard work. David, Paul, and José continually search for ways to better their teaching. In committing to brain-based practices—or any best practices—they realize that they must make efforts to apply them. They recognize, despite perceptions to the contrary, that they are the deciders in their classrooms. They realize that their teaching is largely private and that they are essentially free to decide to incorporate new practices. Whenever they find new approaches that work, they choose to encourage colleagues to try them as well.

Just last week at their book group, David shared a comprehensive approach for using brain-based practices:

> "I received an email from Forest Gingham—you remember him, he used to teach in my department. He told me about the Brain-Targeted Teaching® Model for 21st Century. He decided to take a free online class taught by Dr. Mariale Hardiman, EdD, of Johns Hopkins University. I checked it out and think we ought to consider taking the course

ourselves. We've never taken an online course together. This could be really good!

"Here's the gist: This model, as I discovered on the Hopkins website presents six stages or 'brain targets' of the teaching and learning process. The components include

1. establishing the emotional climate for learning;
2. creating the physical learning environment;
3. designing the learning experience;
4. teaching for the mastery of content, skills, and concepts;
5. teaching for the extension and application of knowledge; and
6. evaluating learning.

"I think this course would help us integrate brain-based teaching into our lessons. And, Kathleen, you'll like this comment from the website: 'A central theme of the model is the integration of the arts to foster retention of new information, conceptual development, and higher-order thinking and creative problem-solving.'" [14]

After considerable discussion and looking on the web, the group agrees to sign up for the course. David says he would be willing to act as facilitator. Given that spring break begins in less than two weeks, once school resumes they agree to begin the course as soon as the course is offered.

The following May, at a Robert Greenleaf brain-based workshop, Paul heard two quotations that directly related to wise and sensitive teaching. The first: "Students are only as safe in your classroom as you are on your worst day." It crystallizes the importance of safe classrooms, one of the tenets that underlie brain research.

If a teacher loses composure with one student, Greenleaf contends, the other students in the class will wait for their turn to receive a similar rebuke. It's difficult to undo the effects of rage, perhaps impossible, Greenleaf says. "I'd better remember this," Paul says to himself.

The other quotation that Greenleaf shared came from Elspeth Campbell Murphy: "If I were a student in my classroom, would I want to return tomorrow?" This powerful adage reminds Paul to pay attention to his teaching from his students' point of view. Greenleaf shared that teachers have put this quotation in their plan book as a daily reminder.[15] Paul intends to do the same—and share both of these aphorisms with his colleagues.

POINTS TO PURSUE

Use brain-research to break away from old habits

One of the temptations of becoming a teacher is that you believe that you will know what to do once you step into your own classroom. After all, you've observed your teachers for sixteen years. Yet, you quickly discover that what worked for you as a student does not work for most of your students.

They are carrying a culture that is less familiar to you. At the same time, you have tools that were not available to your teachers to help you meet your students. Brain research is one of the most effective.

Follow the leads in this chapter and begin to include this valuable research into your lessons. Take one step at a time.

Search the web—and read books

Because of its convenience, Google tempts us to make it our only resource. Yet, we must be wary of its claims, as unvetted sites are more likely to appear than vetted ones. Search the web carefully, seek colleagues' help—and be wary. For deeper study don't forget to read journals and books.

Incorporate exercise into the classroom

While David Thompson's decision to have his students jog around the room may appear extreme, his idea to energize his students merits close attention. John Medina's conclusion, "Physical activity is cognitive candy," deserves to be taken seriously. With obesity on the rise, anything you can do in school and in the classroom to encourage physical movement is a winner. Something as simple as standing up and moving several times during a lesson.

Have students stand up when speaking. Try David Thompson's ideas. Invent your own.

Take seriously the power of naps

Because Paul Ross learned about the importance of naps from John Medina, he is willing to try using them for his early morning high school class. He sees that most of his students are indeed "camels," while he himself is a "lark." Despite resistance from some students—they often find change difficult—and potential pressure from the administration, he introduces naps.

Paul also decides to try power naps in classes when students appeared logy. His middle school colleague, David Thompson, introduces naps for his after-lunch classes, as he wants to test out Medina's idea of the "flatline" time between "camels" and "larks." What will you do about naps in your classroom?

The conundrum of art and music teachers

Art teachers often work from art carts that they wheel from room to room. They teach hordes of students—sometimes up to six hundred—once a week for forty-five minutes and often have them for only one quarter of the year. A similar schedule is often true for music teachers.

How then can teachers in the arts be expected to "boost attention, working memory, and visual-spatial skills, as well as social skills, empathy, timing, patience, verbal memory, and other transferable life skills?" What can you do to change this grievous situation?

Try David Sousa's Primacy-Recency

Primacy-Recency is a concept related to Mary Budd Rowe's 10-2 Thinking. Each points to greater student involvement in the classroom where learning needs to take place. If you tend to teach from the front of the room and find yourself doing most of the talking, emulate José Gonzalez and try Sousa's Primacy-Recency.

To learn about 10-2 Thinking, reread Musad Amur's approach. (See chapter 4, "Lessons: Ambiguity Stimulates Thinking" and the Point to Pursue, "The 10-2 Alternative.") Whichever approach you choose, your students will learn more.

Take an online course together

Have you ever thought of taking an online course with colleagues? For brain research, take a look at the free online class taught by Dr. Mariale Hardiman, Ed.D., of Johns Hopkins University that teaches the Brain-Targeted Teaching® Model for 21st Century. See if the course could work for you and your colleagues. Check the website https://www.coursera.org/ for other a host of other courses.

Establish a dialogue with other teachers with your ideas. Log on to Teachingthatmatters.wordpress.com and join the conversation.

NOTES

1. www.jensenlearning.com/.
2. John Medina, *Brain Rules: 12 Principles for Surviving and Thriving at Work, Home, and School* (Seattle, WA: Pear Press, 2008).
3. David Sousa, *How the Brain Learns* (Thousand Oaks, CA: Corwin, 2001), now in its third edition (2005). The other books in this series are all from Corwin: *How the Brain Learns to Read* (2004); *How the Gifted Brain Learns*; and *How the Special Needs Brain Learns, Second Edition* (2006); *How the Brain Learns Mathematics* (2007); *How the ELL Brain Learns* (2010); *How the Brain Influences Behavior: Management Strategies for Every Classroom* (2009).

4. John Bransford et al., eds., *How People Learn: Brain, Mind, Experience, and School, Expanded Edition* (Washington, DC: National Academy Press, 2000).

5. Ibid., pp. 14–27.

6. John Medina, *Brain Rules*, p. 22.

7. According to Benjamin O. Canada, the superintendent of Atlanta schools, "We are intent on improving academic performance and you don't do that by having kids hang on monkey bars." http://library.adoption.com/articles/no-recess-policies-being-implemented-in-u.s.-school-districts.html

8. Joanna Weiss, "Battling Children's Obesity," *Boston Globe*, September 6, 2011, A11.

9. John Medina, *Brain Rules*, 156–58.

10. Ibid., 158–60.

11. For a thorough explanation of the ten thousand–hour argument, see Malcolm Gladwell, "The 10,000-Hour Rule" in *Outliers: The Story of Success* (New York: Little Brown and Company, 2008), chapter 2.

12. www.jensenlearning.com/.

13. In my adaptation of Sousa's model for workshops, I superimpose a dotted curved line that rises in the center to indicate how most teachers concentrate their instruction during Primacy-Recency's processing time.

14. This website offers excellent online courses for free: https://www.coursera.org/course/braintargeted. A golden opportunity for teachers to collaborate and upgrade their learning.

15. Robert Greenleaf shared these quotations at a keynote at Old Rochester Regional Junior High School, Mattapoisett, Massachusetts, October 28, 2002.

SEVEN
Sabbaths: Take Occasions to Turn Off Electronic Devices

The choice to make the classroom a haven away from the constant chatter of connectivity energizes student-teacher interactions and nourishes long-term learning.

Students come to school with hardly any memory of yesterday's lessons. Every day, they sit in one class after another, after another, after another. Then it's on to sports, clubs, and lessons. Then it's being at home alone. And all through the day their smartphones speak with texts, tweets, Tumblr, and Facebook. The present presses on them only to be forgotten in the next present. They become like the central character in the movie *Memento*,

> unable to remember anything . . . compelled to live moment by moment, without the past ever informing the present. The here and now obliterates the there and then . . . in a society in which the present is unmoored, making anything that happens right now far more important than anything that has happened before.[1]

Students live on incessant sound bites. Texting the message-of-the-moment is instantly important, as just-past messages dissolve into the ether. What's before them counts for everything. They don't remember the past. Perhaps that's why more of them are not doing their homework. It's simply not on their mind.

Henry Wilcox struggles to keep it all straight. An introverted eighth grader with a few friends, he has seven classes a day, including the basics, plus Spanish and woodworking and one period a week of art and PE. Shorter than most of his classmates, he carries a heavy backpack with his textbooks and notebooks—and has a smartphone in his pocket.

By the end of the day, his mind is not only scrambled with the idiosyncrasies of each subject but also by social issues compounded by the emotional demands from texting; during the day he receives texts and clandestinely responds to them during class from his pocket. As he leaves school, he knows that he has four (or is it five?) homework assignments.

Henry's life becomes more complicated. In addition to the usual after-school commitments, today it's soccer, he feels that he has to attend to social media on his smartphone. As he heads to practice and later to his house, Henry texts with friends. He arrives home, procures the key from behind the mailbox, and enters through the front door and relocks it. He goes upstairs to his room, turns on his computer and for the next hour immerses himself on Facebook, mostly trolling for friends, and answers calls and texts on his smartphone.

Today, his mother comes home in time to cook supper. After he eats, he returns to his room and at his mother's urging does some of his homework. He keeps his computer and phone on and sends and responds to more calls, texts, and e-mails. At nine-thirty she reminds him to go to bed. He does what she asks but leaves his phone turned on under his pillow.

Henry Wilcox's teachers are facing new challenges as well. They miss being able to sustain mystery in some of their lessons, as some students may already know what they will say—or find out on Google before the next day's lesson. Fewer students appear willing to work as hard as students used to. Some teachers complain that families believe their kids are simply entitled to good grades. Others notice that students do not care much about school success.

Some teachers blame the fast-paced culture and the fact that students can Google whatever they think they need to know. Why, then, should they pay attention in class? However, some teachers argue that young people may possess new kinds of smarts that are not suitable to the traditional classroom. Henry could well be one of those students.

His teachers perceive him as cooperative but somewhat distracted; one of them suggests he may have ADD. Henry reluctantly participates in groups, as he seems to prefer to work alone or with his good friend Rodger. He also has uncanny ways of seeing through problems, often finding a correct answer, unaware as to how he figures it out. This frustrates his math teacher in particular, as she insists that students show their work.

Henry's language arts teacher, Dan Peterson, sees him differently. He tries to meet Henry and his classmates on their terms. He believes that if he and his colleagues don't meet their students in this fast-changing digital culture, they will become like the frog that sits in gradual warming water and fails to notice that it's coming to a boil until it's too late.

Yet, Dan still struggles to connect with students. He's been teaching middle school language arts for twenty years and has earned a warm reputation with his colleagues, students, and parents. After he completed his master's degree, he wanted to become a writer. Finding it difficult to make a living, he thought that he could share his knowledge and skills with young people.

In his early days in the classroom, his teaching style tended to be reserved and somewhat passive. Being somewhat shy and introspective, he soon realized that his students needed more from him. He began to seek out new ideas and methods that he would try if he thought they had any chance to work.

Now he relentlessly searches for new ideas. Five years ago, at a professional development workshop on Differentiated Instruction (DI), he discovered that DI supports lessons that differentiate (1) content, what students study, (2) learning activities, how they learn, particularly *in* class, and (3) final products, different opportunities to show what they've learned.

Dan also discovered at the workshop that he can design DI lessons that take into account different student readiness levels, interests, or learning styles. While at first he found DI difficult to incorporate, he was convinced from the beginning that it would be more effective than his one-size-fits-all lessons. He was particularly surprised at the impact of student interest as a motivating factor.[2]

For his first foray into differentiating DI products, Dan chooses to try it at the end of his *Catcher in the Rye* unit. Instead of giving a final test, he decides to offer his sixth-period class different product choices to demonstrate what they know and understand. He remembers that day well.

> "It's been quite the three weeks reading and discussing Salinger's *Catcher in the Rye*. You have been wonderfully engaged. I am impressed not only with your analysis of Holden Caulfield's character but also with your comments about his predicaments. Now I want to find out what you know and understand about the book as a whole. Instead of giving you a test, I have decided to offer you different ways to show me what you've learned. Unless you want to work alone, you will choose to do one of them with classmates.
>
> "The choices I've created for you are on this handout. Please follow along as I read.
>
> 1. You can make a **visual** on chart paper that shows me the relationship of Holden to the other characters in the story. The visual should not only indicate who they are but how they relate to him. You do not have to be a good artist to try this.
> 2. Make a **T-chart** on chart paper that lists Holden's positive attributes on one side and his negative ones on the other. After you finish the T-chart, as a group write an explanation for your choices.

3. Imagine that you are chefs who create a **recipe**. Using a recipe format, explain to the 'cook' (reader) the structure and purpose of this novel. Use specific examples.
4. Examine the following **quotation**: 'If you do something too good, then, after a while, if you don't watch it, you start showing off. And then you're not as good any more.' Analyze Holden's words and write how and why they reflect his personality."

After he finished reading, his students began to grumble. Several blurt out their discontent. Dan is surprised at their initial reluctance. After some back and forth comments, he decides to postpone his decision. He knows that metacognitive discussions with his students often prove fruitful—to him and to them. Now is a perfect time. He begins the conversation:

"In this class—and no doubt in others—some of you always do well on tests. Others of you rarely earn A's or B's. But I believe that tests only assess one type of thinking. I think it is important for teachers to offer alternative ways for you to demonstrate your knowledge and understanding. I recall Jackie saying the other day that she finds that tests and quizzes make her nervous. She thinks she knows more than the grades she gets. Right, Jackie? And the same for you, Henry. Right?

"Yes," Jackie replies. "I don't like tests. I like discussions and writing essays much better."

"Me too," says Henry.

"That's why I have prepared these other approaches," Dan replies. "I am not sure that they will work, but I want you to give them a try if you are willing. I want to see if choosing a different product can better demonstrate what you've learned."

Nancy Lipkin, who rarely holds back her thoughts, jumped in. "We always take tests in all of our classes! It's not right not to in your class!"

"You make a good point, Nancy. Those of you who share Nancy's concern can certainly continue to take tests, as I will continue to prepare them. But I believe that eventually schools will allow, perhaps require, alternative ways to assess students. We live in an active digital world, one that demands more creativity and less 'repeativity' (if I can make up such a word).

"I see that the bell is about to ring. We can discuss these ideas again if you like. Meanwhile, tomorrow, I will offer choices along with the usual test. See you then. Good luck!"

At another workshop later in the same year, Dan learns about Understanding by Design (UbD) as a productive approach to plan his curriculum, units, and daily lessons. He's found that his students learn better when he incorporates the three basic premises of backward planning of UbD into his lessons, units, and course of study:

1. when he's explicit about his *desired results* throughout;

2. when he's clear about what *evidence* students need to demonstrate their learning; and
3. when he *plans* well-defined learning experiences.[3]

Dan has replaced his whiteboard with a SMART Board that's connected to his computer. He's found it useful in keeping all students in the loop, particularly if they miss class. Recently, he's incorporated cell phones into his curriculum; once during a class in which his students were writing explanatory papers, he asked them to use their phones to contact a university physicist, one they found on the Internet, and ask his opinion on the significance of the discovery of the Higgs Boson. He was pleased with the responses of the professors—and with his students' animated conversations and essays.

Dan has made good progress with his digitally dependent students, particularly with Henry Wilcox and his buddies, but he knows he has to be inventive if he's to keep up with them. He still uses DI practices that he discovered, as he intends to meet his students where they are in their learning. He divides his lectures (extended talks he calls them) into segments to give time for students to process, an idea he learned from Mary Budd Rowe's research.[4]

Dan continues to be a confirmed "backwards design" aficionado, as he knows that its three principles assure that he and his students are on the same page. He's excited to learn that his school will purchase iPads for all students. He's already planning how to integrate them into his curriculum next year. He's begun to wonder about learning to use Twitter as a way to stay in touch with students; after all, they live comfortably inside social media. Perhaps he should join them.

Every year, Dan makes it his priority to forge close relationships with his students. In the past couple of years, he has noticed that fewer of them speak eye-to-eye to him or to each other. He thinks that as their social-media habits develop, their person-to-person skills may be deteriorating. Despite some of his colleagues claims to the contrary, he feels that social media often drives people apart. He plans to consult with his colleague, Marta McGuinness, who has been teaching her seventh-grade students how to have good conversations.[5]

Taking insights from William Powers's provocative book *Hamlet's Blackberry*, Dan decides to make most of his lessons extended gaps from electronic devices—what Powers calls "Internet Sabbaths." Time away from the incessant demands of social media. Time with no interconnectivity interruptions. No beeps, no blips, no blings, no ringtones. He intends to turn off the PA as well. Dan wants his students to pursue thinking, writing, reflecting, and face-to-face conversations in depth—and with no interruptions.[6]

Dan believes that the classroom may be the last best place in today's culture where students can learn to develop their long-term memories. Where else will they be asked to take extended time away from their electronic devices? Where else will they have time to explore their own minds without interruptions, including the temptation to immediately Google when stuck in their thinking? Where else will they have opportunities to develop essential literacy skills of how to read with pen in hand; how to write, and rewrite; and how to discuss and argue effectively with evidence?[7]

Dan has read Nicholas Carr's *The Shallows*, which also addresses technology's effect on the mind. He was struck with insights that Carr quotes from Jonathan Sweller, an Australian educational psychologist. Sweller argues that long-term memory is essential if humans are to function effectively. Without it, he contends, working memories go on overload and "we become mindless consumers of data."[8] Without long-term memories, people lose the potential to build on the accomplishments of others.

When teachers ask students not to think and only to regurgitate, Dan believes, they deny them any chance to develop their long-term memories. And when they allow students solely to rely on the Internet, students learn to act as receptacles rather than as creators. Unless they develop long-term memories, Dan reflects, they will succumb to living in a history-less world, functioning only in the moment. Certainly the Buddha did not intend "being in the moment" to mean this.

The classroom as the savior of face-to-face human encounters? Teachers as the central actors? Dan Peterson thinks so. So much so that toward the end of the first faculty meeting after spring break, he stands up to speak. Several colleagues look at each other and roll their eyes, as they think they sense what is coming.

> "Are you all aware that humans may have formed many of our language patterns while sitting around campfires on the savannah plains? We have become who we are because we created language in the *presence* of one another. Together humans have built an intricate, complex world of wondrous structures, inventions, and devices that have allowed billions of us to live on this planet, unfortunately not all of us well.
>
> "We need to do all that we can to preserve the gift of human contact. We owe it to our students to teach them how to develop their long-term memories, while at the same time respect the digital world in which they've grown up. After all, we have wonderful connective technologies that keep us in touch with one another. But, will we let them dominate our lives where we find ourselves living moment-to-moment as depicted in the provocative film *Memento*? Will we allow technology to keep us separate from one another?"
>
> George Green stood to make a comment. "Dan, I believe I've heard this from you before." (Dan had a reputation of getting on a soapbox to

advocate his causes.) "Yet, I hear a new urgency in your voice. What's going on?"

"I think I know!" said Fran Lockhart, assistant principal. "Dan is taking the long view of human progress and sees a threat to its trajectory. I have noticed that columnists have been making similar comments. Even in the comics! I have here a "Zippy the Pinhead" that I've saved, as I think its creator, Bill Griffiths, gets it. Listen, it goes like this:

Scenario: A man in a bowler hat with his hands outstretched stands in front of nonsense banners and appeals to a crowd of Pinheads to invite them to come into the big tent behind him.

First Panel: "Yes, ladies and gentlemen, they are oddities of nature . . . yet they live among us . . . on the inside! See the man who never looks up from his smartphone! Watch as he collides with furniture and pedestrians!"

Second Panel: "See the teenager who never speaks, Yes!! She texts her friends hundreds of times a day . . . even . . . get this . . . when they are standing right next to her!"

Third Panel: And strangest of all, ladies and gentlemen . . . the woman who lives not in the present, but in a timeless limbo of streaming video and photos of herself, constantly uploaded to Facebook, Tumblr and Blogspot! It's all on the inside![9]

"You can see, Dan is on to something important! Right Dan?"

"Yes, I am now clear that we are facing a crisis with our students. I think, however, we teachers may be the key to help them realize their potential, perhaps even more than their parents. We have the unique opportunity to help our students develop their capabilities to learn. By learn, I mean to retain what they take in.

"One factor we've not discussed is the lack of sleep that we see in our students. We know that sleep is essential for the brain, so it can process and put what it's learned into long-term memory." Dan reaches into his pocket and takes out some notes.

"In an interview on NPR that I heard recently, Dr. Matthew Walker of the University of California, Berkeley, sleep lab reported: "So [in the brain while sleeping] it's almost like memory pinball—you're bouncing that information around, you're testing which connections to build." Dan added, without having good sleep "after [you've had any] learning, you lose the chance to essentially hit the save button on that information." Besides, he adds, sleep deprivation makes it harder for the brain to regulate emotions.[10] We see the results nearly every day.

"In a conversation that I had after school yesterday with Henry Wilcox," Dan continues, "he shared with me that he and his friends spend more time alone and get less sleep than I did at his age. As I listened, I wondered if the influx of technologies is becoming everyone's decision makers.

"As Fran raised in her "Zippy the Pinhead" example, will personal technologies force the brain to become constantly preoccupied? Will e-mail blings command our thoughts? Will our phones keep us from being present with one another? Yet just last week, two of my students, Fred Liston and Maggie Sherman, told me that they have decided to get off Facebook, as they want to simplify their lives. Maybe there's hope.

"The last point I want to make takes us out of school and onto the street. We see more and more people walking with their heads down, immersed in their smartphones. Are we becoming a culture in which we no longer look into the face of those persons passing us by? Not my choice."

The meeting adjourned. A few colleagues approached Dan to thank him for sharing his ideas. Others left opening their smartphones.

POINTS TO PURSUE

Living without the past

The chapter opens with a reference to *Memento*, a film about a man who has no memory. It serves as a metaphor of how people live today with social media; they tend to act in the moment without reference to the past or thought of the future. Henry Wilcox, an introverted eighth grader, serves as an example of a social-media driven student.

How can you as a teacher help students like Henry to value the importance of continuity, of connecting the past with the present? What will you have to do?

Google as knowledge

Most of us experience the gift of Google nearly every day. It brings us what we want or need to know as soon as we ask. Yet, reliance on Google can short circuit thinking, as it denies opportunities to figure out problems on our own.

What can you do in your classroom to take advantage of Google and at the same time to limit its role to allow for extended thinking to take place—and also find ways to use it to expand critical thinking? Google challenges us to learn to use it well.

Who are today's students?

Your students can be baffling. They seem to come from a different world. They appear to pay less attention. They don't focus on what you say. They fidget, appear uninterested, and at times passive. They certainly are not like you were at their age. You see them immersed in a media that you never knew, which drives their social lives, whether they're connected or not.

You may be aware that if you and your colleagues are not cognizant of the cultural changes affecting the young, as suggested in this chapter, you could drown as a frog in water heading to a boil. What then can you do to attune to your students and become important to them? A crucial question.

Differentiated Instruction

Despite the challenges of this complex methodology, Dan Peterson commits to Differentiated Instruction as a tool to engage his students. Dan is surprised when his students are reluctant to accept alternative ways to be tested.

How do you respond when students struggle with your lessons? If you are interested in trying out DI, seek out the seminal work of Carol Ann Tomlinson; begin with her first book on the subject *The Differentiated Classroom: Responding to the Needs of All Learners* (1999) and explore her website, http://www.caroltomlinson.com, for dozens of resources, including books, articles, videos, presentations, and links to other valuable resources. Seek out a respected professional development DI course, as well.

Understanding by Design

Not long after he started using DI, Dan Peterson discovered Understanding by Design (UbD) at a workshop with Grant Wiggins. UbD has helped him to set desired results for his students, place clear emphasis on evidence for learning, and plan a clear sequence of lessons. He recommends the website http://www.authenticeducation.org for an introductory explanation, books, and resources.

His favorite educational book is Carol Ann Tomlinson and Jay McTighe's (Wiggins's partner) *Integrating Differentiated Instruction and Understanding by Design* (2006), which ties together both of these valuable strategies.

Respond actively to the digital culture

How do you visualize your classroom in today's digitally driven culture? If you've been an educator for more than ten years, you may have taken time to reassess your role in light of these developments. What have you discovered?

Do you use a SMART Board? Do you use cell phones? What other electronics do you use? Are you aware of how technologies have helped students with disabilities? Have you avoided using some technologies?

Invoke "Internet Sabbaths"

Do you agree with Dan Peterson's contention that classrooms may be the savior of face-to-face human encounters? Have you discussed with students the value of personal conversation without having access to texting? Are you willing to publicly state that you take "Internet Sabbaths" for the purpose of thinking and talking together about what matters?

What can you do to implement such Sabbaths? How patient and willing are you to wait for good results? What will you say to those who call you a "Luddite"? Perhaps you could show them your favorite apps that you're an expert at using.

Make long-term learning a priority

Dan, like many of his colleagues, notices that students seem to retain less and less of what he teaches. At first, he thinks it might be his teaching methods—and he believes he was right. But he also realizes that now he may be dealing with more complex issues.

After he shared at the faculty meeting what he heard on NPR about the brain and sleeping, he became convinced that he and his colleagues need to do all they can to build long-term memory into their teaching. What can you do to make long-term learning central to your teaching? What might you suggest to Dan?

Establish a dialogue with other teachers with your ideas. Log on to Teachingthatmatters.wordpress.com and join the conversation.

NOTES

1. Neil Gabler, "Constant information–and nothing remembered," *Boston Globe*, November 26, 2009. His reference to *Memento* refers to the 2000 film in which a man suffers from severe short-term memory loss. http://www.boston.com/bostonglobe/editorial_opinion/oped/articles/2009/11/26/constant_information___and_nothing_remembered/?.

2. Google Carol Ann Tomlinson for a plethora of articles and works on Differentiated Instruction.

3. Google Grant Wiggins at www.authenticeducation.org to learn more about Backwards Design.

4. See chapter 4 "Lessons: Create Ambiguity to Stimulate Thinking" for Musad Amur's implementation of 10-2 Thinking.

5. See chapter 5, "Conversation: Make Time for Reflective Talking and Listening."

6. William Powers, *Hamlet's Blackberry: A Practical Philosophy for Building the Good Life in the Digital Age* (New York: HarperCollins, 2010).

7. Michael Schmoker, *Results Now: How We Can Achieve Unprecedented Improvement in Teaching and Learning* (ASCD 2006). See chapter 6, "Authentic Literacy and Intellectual Development," 58–75 for an articulate discussion of the rigors of literacy and its place in the classroom.

8. Jonathan Sweller in Nicolas Carr, *The Shallows: What the Internet is Doing to Our Brains* (New York: W.W. Norton & Company), 123–26.

9. Bill Griffth, "Zippy the Pinhead," "Freak Show," September 20, 2013.

10. "'Memory Pinball' and Other Reasons You Need a Nap," NPR *Weekend Edition Sunday*, September 8, 2013.

EIGHT

Symphony: Teach to the Whole Child

One note of a symphony hints at its potential, but all the notes bring it to life — the same holds true for teaching.

When Joe Effinger was hired to teach ancient history in middle school, he knew that he could not begin with the Sumerians at the Fertile Crescent. He was convinced that at Mesopotamia, humans had already established farming, government, writing, and economic, social, and religious institutions. He wanted his students to understand how humans evolved for nearly two million years before developing civilization.

Joe and his students have become fascinated with the human hunter-gatherer heritage. For about two hundred thousand years, early humans migrated out of Africa in nomadic groups of fifteen to thirty people. Their lifestyle remained the same through countless generations.

Then suddenly, so it seems, thirty-two thousand years ago, sophisticated cave paintings appeared at Chauvet in the Ardeche Valley of France. And by ten thousand years ago, humans had created civilizations in Sumer, Egypt, the Indus Valley, and the Americas. No doubt, more evidence from these early years of human cultural evolution awaits discovery.

Joe wonders with his students,

- "What makes us humans distinctive on this planet?"
- "Who are we?"
- "What urged our ancestors, hunter-gatherers, to move beyond their survival, animal-style living and become more sophisticated?"
- "How did language emerge?"
- "What nudged early humans to create magnificent cave paintings?"

Today, as cultural speed confronts the planet every day, humans face the issue of biological versus cultural evolution. As for hunter-gatherers, their cultural speed must have remained nearly at zero for generations. But, since the discovery of the exquisite drawings at Chauvet, Joe sees a culture already speeded up. He sees that humans now must face cultural speed and its part in the future. He and his students wonder what drives some cultures to conserve and others to push for change.

He asks his students such questions as:

- Why does global culture speed faster than people seem able to comprehend?
- How is this culture redefining who we are?
- Who controls the expansion of culture?
- Will cultural evolution replace biological evolution?
- And, is destruction built in to human behavior as it is in the greater universe?

~ ~ ~

Christopher McDougall's intriguing book *Born to Run* gives serious consideration to hunter-gatherer culture.[1] Underneath his fascinating tale of the world's greatest ultra-marathon runners, the Tarahumara Indians of Mexico's Copper Canyons, McDougall seeks to find out how we became the human beings we are today. He cites the research of Dennis Bramble, David Carrier, and Louis Liebenberg. They all want to know how *Homo sapiens* (Running Man) was able to displace the Neanderthals and emerge triumphant after the Ice Age, about forty-five thousand years ago. Liebenberg revitalizes our thinking about the significance of hunter-gatherer culture:

> How did we leap from basic survival thinking, like that of other animals, to wildly complicated concepts like logic, humor, deduction, abstract reasoning, and creative imagination? Okay, so primitive man upgraded his hardware with a bigger brain—*but where did he get the software?* . . . *So where did that spark of inspiration come from?*[2] (Italics are mine.)

Liebenberg wanted to test his theory that Running Man's modern intelligence emerged from his ability to outrun animals. He decided to travel to the Kalahari Desert in southern Africa to run down kudus, a large antelope, with traditional Bushman tribal hunters.[3] After he confirmed his theory, the question as to how Running Man got the software remains a mystery. A fascinating account!

That we evolve is natural law. Where we will get to—wherever that is—is another question. We have the power and, unfortunately, inclination to eliminate ourselves with nuclear war, ecological disaster, corruption, climate change, or overpopulation. Or a renegade asteroid may hit the earth. Nevertheless, astronomers inform us that the universe will eventually exercise its destructive/creative forces and eliminate our home on the edge of the Milky Way Galaxy. Earth will cease well before the sun dies in approximately five billion years. We live in precious times.

These musings relate to the provocative writing of Brian Swimme and Thomas Berry. In their seminal work *The Universe Story*, they describe the universe as having at all levels *differentiation, communion,* and *autopoiesis*. Their comment on one-dimensionality is particularly poignant:

> For knowledge of understanding to be reduced to one-dimensionality—as with certain scientific tendencies to reduce all knowledge to the quantitative mode—would be similar to reducing a whole symphony to a single note. An integral relationship with the universe's differentiated energy constellations requires a multivalent understanding that includes the full spectrum of modes of knowing.[4]

~ ~ ~

In 1980, Sarah Johansen, a junior in college and a late convert to history as a major, becomes intrigued with the universe perspective after she sees Carl Sagan's *Cosmos* series on television. She decides then that she wants to become a high school social studies teacher. She commits to center her teaching around the human's place in the universe. She hopes that her students would find this perspective intriguing.

When she reads Berry and Swimme twelve years later, she discovers that she is teaching students, each of whom has *differentiation, communion*, and *autopoiesis*. She sees each of her students as complex and *different*; each with the capacity to connect and *communicate*; and each *self-generating* as a discoverer, creator, inventor, and designer.[5] She realizes that by holding this vision she is teaching to the whole symphony of each student.

Now in her thirtieth year in the classroom, she finds herself struggling against pressure from school authorities to narrow the focus of student achievement to solely test scores. In recent faculty meetings, Sarah has raised serious questions with her colleagues about her concerns. At a February meeting, with the support of her principal, Morton Lawrence, she projects the following questions from her iPad onto a big-screen TV:

1. Will a focus on test results force us to teach to only one note of the full symphonies that students bring? Will we, then, create national clones of trained test takers?
2. When we make test success the goal of education, what kind of students will we send to the next levels—and eventually perhaps even to an Ivy League school?

3. Will narrow-focus, résumé-building, test-prep indoctrination hinder our students from personal exploration, discovery, and creativity?
4. Will our students be prepared to take advantage of the full spectrum of human possibilities when they arrive at university or join the workforce?
5. Will the focus on testing curtail students' potential? If so, can they recover?

Principal Lawrence thanks Sarah for her questions. He wants the faculty to explore their implications in small groups at the next meeting. He asks Sarah, then, to ask her colleagues for their initial impressions.

Martin Jenisch decides to chime in. He's been an articulate and insightful member of Sarah's department and an early protester against the current emphasis on testing. He's taught nearly as long as Sarah and is well-known for his creative teaching. His students express appreciation for his flexibility and imaginative methods. He states:

> "If we decide to teach to each child's self-generative, unique self—in the words of Brian Swimme and Thomas Berry, to put their "whole symphony" in play—we will certainly face a conundrum: We may well shortchange the honing of test-prep skills that are deemed necessary for each rung of the ladder of test success, beginning in the first grade. We could, some might say, deny them admission to Harvard!
>
> "Still," Martin continues, "I choose to play to the whole symphony! I accept Philip Pullman's appeal: 'We should act *as if* the universe were listening to us and responding. We should act as if we were going to win.'[6] I choose the full-engagement paradigm, the whole symphony. The whole enchilada. Every day. Nothing less will do!"

For a brief moment, one could hear a pin drop. Martin has expressed an understated truth that several others immediately understand. Jordan Norris, one of the school's guidance counselors, who is well respected by staff and students, stands to speak.

> "Contrary to conventional wisdom, the full-engagement teaching that Martin is talking about does *not* hinder test success. I've observed teachers in this school who choose not to treat students as receptacles.
>
> "They ask them to think critically; wrestle with what matters; problem solve; probe real issues; become creative; explore ancient wisdom; develop sustained attention; converse openly; care deeply; and become active in the presence of one another. . . . All these and more make for full human beings—and most likely at the same time assure that students will indeed pass those pesky tests!"

Several nod in agreement. The discussion becomes animated. After several others offered their ideas, Joe Camden, a quiet, unassuming biology teacher, who has taught at the school for a dozen years, stood to share his perceptions.

"Along with Sarah, I, too, have been using the Swimme-Berry perspective in my science classes. My students find their story of the emerging universe intriguing. I'd like, then, to propose further questions that we might consider as a faculty. Let me share them:

1. What parts of our students' whole symphonies are we stifling by our obsession with testing?
2. How might our focus on data-driven testing deny our students access to their other notes?
3. If we continue to focus on testing, how will our students' personal seeds, their emerging calling, be blockaded?
4. And, will testing stunt our students, as happens to trees when they are pruned too early?"

Again the room becomes quiet. Morton Lawrence asks Joe to give him a copy of his questions to include them along with Sarah's for consideration at the next meeting. Then Sarah stands to offer her final thoughts:

"No one can become whole without practice at being whole. If we deliver a narrow education, we will produce narrow people. We can choose Socrates or drill-and-kill test prep. If we intend to develop full human beings, I believe the choice is obvious."

~ ~ ~

The ultra-marathoner Tarahumara Indians make this choice. They choose not to participate in races for recognition and rewards. They choose not to wear expensive shoes that hurt the feet. They choose not to engage in repetitive rituals for training.

Instead, they learn to run by kicking barefoot a wooden ball down rugged paths as they jump over rocks, roots, and water. The whole symphony of their bodies and minds is engaged—and they do it for sheer pleasure.[7] How remarkable if schools were to choose to emulate the Tarahumaras' physical intelligence and playful sense of humor. What remarkable symphonies would emerge!

We humans not only have consciousness but are also conscious of our consciousness. We can look to the past or to the future and put ourselves in either place. We think moon, and we are there. We visualize our planet at the edge of the Milky Way, and we are there. Our forebears emerged from the African savannah to create civilizations. Today we can see and speak to anyone anywhere on the planet.

Teachers can choose to join Sarah Johansen, Martin Jenisch, and their colleagues and invite students to discover this perspective of the universe. They might begin by sharing the astronauts' view of our remarkable blue earth from space, what Carl Sagan called the "pale blue dot."[8]

Humans have come a long way from their hunter-gatherer heritage. Joe Effinger and his middle school students appreciate the role that the hunter-gatherer way of life has played in human development. As part of their inquiry, they explore questions, such as:

- "What urged some hunter-gatherer forebears to become unstuck from thousands of years of living in packs?"
- "What was their sense of consciousness?"
- "What biological evolution has emerged in humans since then?"
- And one of Joe's favorites: "Is Ray Kurzweil's concept of singularity, which states that humans will some day merge with technology, become evolution's next step?"

Culturally, humans are hurtling toward unknowns. Unlike previous generations, they can no longer anticipate the next generation's priorities, possibilities, and problems—although some, including Joe, try.

POINTS TO PURSUE

The challenge of cultural change

This chapter offers a perspective on our human origins. It begins with Joe Effinger's decision to teach ancient history by initially focusing on hunter-gatherer culture. It explores the transition from this culture to the present and notes that today's biological human faces rapid cultural change.

It also suggests that teachers should be cognizant of today's constant cultural change, most obvious in technology, and make efforts to help students better understand the world in which they live—and where they've come from.

What might you say to your students about cultural speed and cultural continuity? Do you believe that schools have a responsibility to address this issue? What do your colleagues think?

Ask big questions

"Okay, so primitive man upgraded his hardware with a bigger brain—but where did he get the software? . . . So where did that spark of inspiration come from?" asks Louis Liebenberg in this chapter.

Do you wish sometimes that schools focused their curriculums around such unanswerable questions? Do you wish that you could listen to the minds of your students exploring such questions? Do you wish that education was less about providing input and more about bringing out what's inside students so they can explore and imagine?

Given the constraints of your curriculum, what do you do to encourage students' larger thinking? What can you do to bring out student curiosity in your classroom?

Our universe connection

Sarah Johansen is one of many teachers who appear in this book. Each one of them has a personal history, each brings her unique self into her school, each is her own person.

When you speak of yourself as a teacher, you may well forget how different you are. Yet, as Brian Swimme and Thomas Berry make clear, you are not only complex and different, but you also have the capacity to communicate and can discover, create, invent, and design. What's also important, these characteristics belong to all creatures in the universe.

How can you as a teacher, then, give your students this larger global sense and at the same time encourage them to grow into their unique selves? Whether you are a primary school teacher or college professor, what is your role in this process? Should you even take time to think and act at this level?

The limits of testing

At the faculty meeting described in this chapter, Sarah and her colleague Joe Camden ask provocative questions that relate to the limitations of testing and test scores. Sarah's five questions point to the detrimental effect of focusing on test results; Joe's questions build on Sarah's and center on his concern that testing limits students from fulfilling their whole-symphony selves.

How do you respond to their questions? Do you connect with them? Have you thought about the lasting effects of the emphasis of testing on your students? Are their questions worth asking in your school? Do you teach your students to be whole-symphony beings? Do you see yourself as a whole-symphony teacher and person?

The future of humans

What do you think of Ray Kurzweil's concept of "singularity" (the merging of humans with technology) as evolution's next step? We already replace body parts with prostheses and produce internal organs with 3D printers. Do you think that Kurzweil's prediction will eventually happen? Then what will "being human" mean? Is such a "being" even imaginable?

What would your students say about these ideas? And, do you agree that we are now "hurtling towards unknowns . . . we can no longer anticipate the next generation's priorities"? If you agree, do you need to rethink what you teach, how you teach, and why you teach?

Establish a dialogue with other teachers with your ideas. Log on to Teachingthatmatters.wordpress.com and join the conversation.

NOTES

1. Christopher MacDougall, *Born to Run: A Hidden Tribe, Superathletes, and the Greatest Race the World Has Never Seen* (New York: Vintage, 2011).
2. Ibid., 233.
3. Ibid., 233–39. Truly fascinating!
4. Brian Swimme and Thomas Berry, *The Universe Story: From the Primordial Flaring Forth to the Ecozoic Era—A Celebration of the Unfolding of the Cosmos* (HarperCollins, 1992), 74.
5. Ibid., 71–3.
6. Laura Miller, "Far From Narnia: Philip Pullman's Secular Fantasy for Children," *The New Yorker*, December 26, 2005 and January 1, 2006, 3.
7. Christopher MacDougall, *Born to Run.* The Tarahumara Indians are featured throughout the book.
8. Carl Sagan, *Pale Blue Dot: A Vision of the Human Future in Space* (New York: Balantine Books, 1997).

NINE
Recruit: Make Schools Safe for All Students

A school-wide safety net assures the each student feels that he or she belongs to the school community.

Adrian Waters wanted to teach since she was five. She often played school with her friends and always saw herself as the teacher. Now a recent college graduate who double majored in English and education, she can hardly wait to meet her ninth and eleventh grade language arts classes.

At workshops with her fellow new teachers before school opens, she contributes to discussions on how she intends to make a difference with students. They all agree on one point: not to replicate the traditional ways in which most of their teachers taught. They are excited to make learning engaging for their students.

By the third day of school, the optimistic, energetic, and perky Adrian is overwhelmed. One hundred twenty-two students and three preps! How will she keep up? When she meets her friend Alice Sorenson, who teaches second grade, she learns that Alice, too, is feeling overwhelmed. Alice spends the whole day with hardly a break with her twenty-nine students—and teaches all subjects. "Nobody prepared us for this, did they?" says the usually calm and collected Alice.

Despite early frustrations, Adrian and Alice are learning to know their students. As for their names, Alice finds it easier, as she has only twenty-nine. Adrian, on the other hand, struggles to learn the names of her one hundred twenty-two students, particularly because matching names to faces is challenging for her. Besides, like other new teachers, she finds herself focusing more on her lessons than on individual students.

By early in the second week, Adrian begins to see them less as a group and more as individuals. She's confident that she is finally learning nearly all of their names. Some names come easily, particularly those of students have been in her face from the first day.

She is surprised, however, to suddenly see Juan, who sits toward the back of the room and has been in her second period class for several days. She hasn't noticed him before. She asks herself, "Why haven't I seen him?" How has he slipped into the woodwork? How has he avoided me? Then she remembers learning about the "gray kids" who blend in with everyone. She, too, was like that.[1] Whenever she was in a group, she preferred to wait for the right moment to make herself known.

Robert Kegan, Harvard psychologist, offers a profound perspective on perceiving students. In his seminal work *The Evolving Self* he introduces the concept of "recruitability." He describes babies whom nature provides with the natural gift of recruiting. Hardly anyone can resist a baby's eyes, despite the large head, huge forehead, and little body.

On the other hand, nature is not so kind later on. As people grow older they do not have equal abilities to recruit. Adolescents are a case in point. Some are more "attractive" than others. Some naturally invite people into their lives, while others push people away. Some slip into the woodwork.

Healthy, well-fed babies in orphanages have been known to die because of their failure to recruit an adult. They lie in their cribs deprived of human contact. Making personal connections, apparently, is essential to life. Kegan connects this concept to schools:

> The greatest inequalities in education are not between schools . . . but within them; that greater than the inequalities of social class or achievement test scores is *the unequal capacity of students to interest others in them*—a phenomenon not reducible to social class or intelligence, and which seems to be the more powerful determinant of future thriving.[2] (Italics are mine.)

Kegan asks teachers to recruit and be recruitable. They need to be open to all of their students, not only to those who lure them into their web. They need to become open to those who fail to reach out for attention. Schools have to be sure that each and every student is recruited, that each one is held by at least one staff person whom the student knows and cares about. All students deserve to feel that they belong.

At first, as Adrian discovers, new teachers may not be ready to take into account Kegan's recruitability mindset, as they are busy trying to claim their space. They can barely keep up. They feel pressure to focus on what they need to teach, regardless of knowing that "I'm supposed to be here for the kids." They struggle to connect with all of them.

As a new teacher, Adrian is like a mother sitting beside her child on an airplane. When oxygen masks drop down, as the flight attendant instructs, the mother is to put her mask on first before she puts one on her child. So too in the classroom. Adrian, who works alone, has to care for herself first, to keep her wholeness amid the chaos of the first days and weeks.

As she becomes more comfortable, she is better able to focus on all of her students—each and every one of them. She's ready to "put on" their masks, ready to recruit them all. In Kegan's words, she's ready to level the playing field of "the unequal capacity of students to interest others in them."

Veteran teachers need to take Kegan's insight to heart. Whether they admit it or not, they like some students better than others, as they may say (privately) that they have favorites. Yet they need to take responsibility for recruiting each and every one. Teachers know that a student who attempts to disappear right in front of them may actually be pleading for recognition. When teachers find a way to that student, it makes a difference to him or her—and to everyone.

Ultimately, recruitment is a school-wide responsibility. Brian Flanagan, the flamboyant former principal of Somersworth (New Hampshire) High School, developed a system that recruited every student. He required that each teacher who led a club or team to become the safety net for those students. He and his vice principal, Carl Fitzgerald, took responsibility for those students who were not in clubs or on teams and met with them at lunchtime. Thus, all the students in the school were held accountable. They knew that they belonged.[3]

In school communities that recruit all students, bullying is curtailed. When everyone belongs, everyone feels safe.

POINTS TO PURSUE

New teacher conundrum

New teachers anticipate their first days with optimism. They believe that they can step in and make a positive difference from the first day. Yet, as we see in this chapter from Adrian Waters and Ann Sorenson, such is often not the case. Wanting to be everything for their students, they find themselves having to cope with unexpected challenges and disappointments—including the struggle to learn students' names.

Do you remember such predicaments? What can you do to help new teachers on your staff, especially if you don't have a mentoring program? What is your responsibility for others on your staff?

Recruit every student

How do you react to Robert Kegan's contention that "the greatest inequalities in education are not between schools . . . but within them?" Do you believe this inequality is true in your school?

Begin with yourself: Take an inventory of your students. Have you recruited them all? How well do you know each of them? How do you find out about those who try to hide? How can you let each student know that you know who they are and care about them? If you cannot reach a student, do you know who has?

Do you know if your colleagues are aware of Kegan's concept of recruitability?

Build community through recruitability

Once you understand the central importance of recruitability in your classroom, what can you do to teach students to be recruitable for one another? How can you help build true community where students know and respect each other? What can you do to take leadership in this process?

Do you believe that bullying would be curtailed in school communities in which all students have been recruited?

Build school-wide safety nets

In this chapter Brian Flanagan and Carl Fitzgerald developed a system that recruited every student in their high school. Every student was held in a safety net. Students knew that they belonged. How well does your school know its students? How well does it provide a safety net for each of them?

Establish a dialogue with other teachers with your ideas. Log on to Teachingthatmatters.wordpress.com and join the conversation.

NOTES

1. I first learned of the term "gray kids" from Lavinia Ruiz, who was one herself.
2. Robert Kegan, *The Evolving Self: Problem and Process in Human Development* (Cambridge MA: Harvard University Press, 1982), 15ff.
3. Personal conversation with Brian Flanagan and Carl Fitzgerald.

II

Seek New Perspectives

> It is what it is. —Anonymous

Wisdom from outside sources opens educators to new thinking.

Part II invites teachers to make it their intention to discover alternative ways to engage students and themselves.

When a teacher listens to her teaching, sudden insights may occur. Occasionally they stick, other times they don't. Sometimes, she shares an insight during a lesson that takes the class to unexpected places. Some students enjoy her improvisational style, while others prefer her to stay on task. When she reveals her penchant for jokes and punning, it delights some and frustrates others. She never knows how classes will react until they settle into their own chemistry.

Insights arrive in her mind as she wakes up. In the shower. On a walk. While reading. Most anywhere. Some stick, others slip into the ether, only to reemerge later. Often they come from unexpected places.

In her early years of teaching, she read Scott Peck's *The Road Less Traveled*. Its first sentence "Life is difficult" has marinated in her mind ever since. It led her to understand that teaching, too, is difficult—and not simply hard work with long hours. By accepting difficulty, it no longer becomes difficult.[1] At least, not as difficult. In her mind, it is what it is.

Without her pursuit of insights, she knows that her teaching becomes mundane, routine, and ineffective. Insights lead to new understandings. When she puts them into play, whether successful or not, her teaching renews and her students benefit. Together in a new space, she and her students seek to understand "it is what it is."

The four essays in chapter 10, "In the Classroom," seek to discover "it is what it is" inside the school experience. The first essay compares yellow school buses and metro minibuses as metaphors for teaching; the second assesses the impact of a then-unique process to enrich student word processing; the third speculates on the value of Dilbert's irreverent sensibility; and the last explores the notion of how portals can lead students out into the larger world.

The four essays in chapter 11, "Beyond the Classroom," offer insights from sources outside schools. The first essay explores the mind of the Internet from the perspective of the universe; it brings in wisdom from Brian Swimme and Thomas Berry, as well as Bill McKibben and Carl Sagan. The second essay explores the essential power of nonaction from three different sources: a *Boston Globe* columnist's observations, a Unitarian minister's sermon, and writer Benjamin Hoff's account of the irrepressible Winnie the Pooh.

The final two essays offer perspectives that can be gained from incidents with common items: in this case, car keys and a paper cutter.

NOTE

1. M. Scott Peck, *The Road Less Traveled: A New Psychology of Love, Traditional Values and Spiritual Growth* (New York: Touchstone, 1978), 15.

TEN

In the Classroom

The four essays in this chapter invite educators to think outside the box to expand their thinking and practice.

A METAPHOR EVOKES CLARITY: PUT STUDENT LEARNING FIRST

Allison Brentwood's decision to drive a metro minibus rather than a yellow school bus signifies her commitment to pay attention to what her students learn.

Teaching is difficult. Once a teacher understands that teaching must first be about what her students actually learn rather than about what she teaches, she faces a conundrum. Does she align with her colleagues and deliver lessons on the pacing schedule that they've decided at the department meeting? Or does she consider departing from the planned schedule and take more time to assure that all of her students are learning?

Allison Brentwood faces this conundrum. When thinking about becoming a teacher, Allison believed that her innate curiosity would be a catalyst for her students. In college, she was known as a philosophical maverick who frequently connected seemingly unrelated ideas.

Now in her tenth year teaching high school social studies, she has been wrestling with this conundrum ever since she first considered letting go of thinking of teaching less as delivery and more as immersion. She has made it a habit from her first year to seek better ways to connect with her students. Her colleagues know her as somewhat unconventional but a team player nevertheless.

One of her many innovative approaches was her unit on Chinese philosophy that resulted in a class publication, a ten-page, four-inch-by-five-inch mini-booklet she entitled "'The Wisdom of Confucius: As Written by His Devoted Disciples,' Under the Tutelage of Allison-ti." In it were seventy-six student analects emulating Confucius. For the booklet, she decided to give each student a Chinese name derived from their own name and place it in front of their analect. Three examples:

> Trev-Mar said to Confucius while driving him past a village, "The man who believes all that he hears without question is the inferior man."
>
> Cait-lin, a whimsical disciple of Confucius who loved to run in the woods, quipped, "In a race it is more fun to beat the boys than to draw hearts around their names."
>
> Matt Shao, a devoted disciple of Confucius, suddenly sat up and spoke: "The old man who is wise is rich, for wisdom is more precious than all the gold in the world."

One evening, as she considers how to focus more directly on what her students are learning *during* classes, she has an insight: "Teaching is a choice," she says to herself. "Thinking metaphorically, either I could drive a traditional yellow school bus or drive a modern metro-style minibus." She writes in her journal:

> If I persist in *delivery*—to cover material—I would be choosing to drive a yellow school bus filled with students who sit in rows on both sides of the aisle. I check to see if everyone is in their seat. I specify what I want them to see along the road. As the bus departs, I turn on the PA so everyone can hear me. I drive the bus along a well-marked curriculum path that anticipates my lesson plan and that aims to arrive at each stop on time. Most days, the bus reaches its intended destination. On the days it doesn't, I make it up the next day.
>
> But, if I were to *engage* students—to put learning first—I would be choosing instead to drive a metro minibus with informal-style seating. As students enter, I greet them by name. They sit face to face. I drive the bus on a road that serves as a guide, an intention, but in no way is the route foreordained. As forks and sidetracks appear, I pay attention to my students' observations.
>
> Sometimes I turn the bus to the right, sometimes to the left, or continue straight on. I may stop to allow my students to savor where they are, or I may decide to retrace our path so they might better understand where we are headed. I bring the bus to a meaningful destination but not always to the one intended.
>
> I will choose the minibus.

Allison realizes that her decision will put pressure on her from school officials and colleagues. The administration's relentless focus on meeting the challenges of outside assessments may tempt her to reconsider and decide to drive the yellow school bus just to keep up. She already feels somewhat negated in the teaching process, as the administration allows her hardly any say in what to teach.

Allison also resents having to wait months for test results about her students' success because she used to ascertain their progress herself—clear evidence in her mind of society's growing lack of trust in teachers' judgment.

It takes courage for a teacher to break away from this tyranny of top-down pressure that trains narrow-thinking, one-note students and, instead, decide to take the alternative choice to nurture them as whole-symphony human beings.[1]

Allison's choice to take the wheel of the metro minibus will most likely distance her from most of her colleagues. Certainly, she will not receive kudos from them, nor will she seek their praise. As her independence becomes more obvious, she will undoubtedly feel more alone. Yet in her heart she'll be following deeply held principles that she has about being a teacher. She will maintain her integrity.

She knows the temptation to drive the yellow school bus lies deep in teachers' psyches and makes them feel safe, as it used to for her. It means to follow an approved delivery-based, test-oriented curriculum that leaves little time for engagement. It means being a part of the school's culture. It means feeling safe and assures a future contract.

Why then does Allison make the choice to drive the metro minibus? The obvious answer, she concludes, is that she has to do it for her students and their families—and she knows that it's the right thing to do, practically and spiritually.

Yet, she wonders if she will be able to sustain her decision. She wonders if she may occasionally need to step back into the yellow bus. "I know that it will be hard to separate myself from my colleagues," she says to herself, "but at the same time, I may have to stay in the game on their terms. That way, I may have a better chance to keep my job. But, if I persist on my new path, I may have a chance to convince some of them to join me."

One evening as she reflects on her decision, she realizes that now she can let go of commonly embedded poor practices that exert authority rather than invite learning. Such practices, she notes in her journal:

> No longer will I have to insert rote knowledge and skills into the minds of unsuspecting students. No longer will I insist that they copy down whatever I say just because I say it. No longer will I have to race through material, give quizzes and a unit test, and then move directly to the next unit, even when some students have not learned the current material. And, no longer will I have to pretend that all students who come to my classes are well prepared.

Allison inspires her students to remember what happens in class. She's always been like that. During discussions she respects their ideas by putting them on the board. She incorporates a SMART Board, because its interactive qualities engage her students. And because it connects to her computer, she can record her lessons and provide continuity for those who are absent.

Recently, she asked her colleague, Jesse Patterson, who is the school's wizard with the Internet, to design a website to make her assignments accessible to students and to inform parents. And she teaches with a mindset that seeks to know who her students are and what they are learning—and she makes every effort to listen more than talk.

Later, she writes in her journal:

> I am grateful that I now commit first to my students. I know that some of my department colleagues are annoyed because I resist sticking with the preplanned curriculum, but I am convinced that all my students must have the time they need to learn.
>
> Some teachers have questioned why I do not come to the faculty room during my planning periods. I tell them that I am researching for my classes, but I really don't want to listen to their complaints about the administration, other teachers, and students.
>
> I like that I have made my teaching more active and more engaging. My students recognize that I work hard to gain their attention and respect—and that I encourage them to work hard as well. I hope that someday colleagues will choose to come to see what I am doing and give me feedback.
>
> I know that my decision not to teach to tests is right. If I teach literacy skills thoroughly and consistently—to read with pen in hand, to think and write with rigor, and to develop argumentative skills—I will prepare my students to succeed on any tests.[2]
>
> I am convinced, as a twenty-first-century teacher, that I have to reach beyond teaching meaningful content. I also need to focus on communication skills, critical thinking, performance abilities, and depth of knowledge and understanding. I know, too, that I have to partner with my students in assessing their learning. And, I am sure that if I am able to talk less and listen more, they will become even more engaged.

After Allison finds the courage to make the choice to drive the metro minibus, she becomes confident that she is taking a less-traveled road to serve her students well. She understands, however, that if she were to revert to deliver curricula at a set pace, to make no effort to observe colleagues, and not invite them to observe her, she would condone the school's culture of isolation—and remain on the yellow school bus.

POINTS TO PURSUE

Teachers' conundrum

Allison Brentwood, the high school social studies teacher in this chapter, has the courage to face what all teachers must face whether they acknowledge it or not: whether to cover material on time or focus on what students are actually learning.

Using her journal, she discovers the yellow-bus/metro-minibus metaphor and decides that she will drive the minibus. At the same time, she recognizes that her decision may well separate her from colleagues and administrators who prefer to work traditionally. Still, she makes the commitment.

Where do you fall on the spectrum of Alison's conundrum? Do you lean one way or the other? Are you willing to commit to drive the minibus and trudge through the hurdles that you may encounter? Or, do you prefer the yellow school bus?

Making a case

Once Allison makes her commitment, she takes time to assess. In one journal entry, she lists common poor practices that she no longer intends to use. She also notes her decision to incorporate a SMART Board and create a classroom website. In another entry, she lists all the ways that her new commitment is making a difference to her and to her students.

What do you think of her arguments in support of driving the minibus? What practices might you need to change to make it more possible to connect with the gifts and strengths of your students? Will writing a journal help?

Establish a dialogue with other teachers with your ideas. Log on to Teachingthatmatters.wordpress.com and join the conversation.

Chapter 10

THE POWER OF MACRO KEYS: MAKE REWRITING NECESSARY

Fred Olson's decision to use technology to engage with his students' writing assures that they will rewrite.

It is 1984. Fred Olson teaches eighth-grade social studies. He's been a teacher for nearly twenty-five years. He brings his energetic self into his classroom every day. He usually wears a jacket and tie and jeans. Despite his reputation as a free thinker and practitioner, he is always Mr. Olson to his students, even in those years in the 1970s when most of his colleagues chose to be called by their first names.

Fond of new ideas, he imagines Apple's new Macintosh as a potential game changer for his teaching. He has yet to own a computer. His brother Peter, who is at graduate school, has an opportunity to purchase the Macintosh at a special university price. As Peter has no interest in owning it, he agrees to buy it and resell it to Fred.

As soon as the Macintosh arrives, Fred can hardly contain himself. He opens its Picasso box and slowly lifts out the 128K state-of-the-art tan computer, keyboard, and mouse. From a second box, he takes out an ImageWriter printer, a serial hard drive, and a small box of three-and-one-half-inch floppy disks. He plugs in the computer and turns it on. A dual-face, line-drawn image slowly materializes in the middle of the nine-inch monochrome display screen. He beams.

Soon he has his first revelation. After using to the manual to set up his Macintosh, he discards it, as he easily navigates its menu. Before long, he becomes one with his Macintosh. The manual collects dust.

When Fred realizes that he can easily read and edit his writing, he smiles again. Finally others will actually be able to read what he writes! He gave up using a typewriter years before, as he erased as much as he typed. Despite tapping with only two fingers on his keyboard, he finds a new sense of freedom. Now he does not have to ask Donna, the faculty secretary, to struggle to interpret his handwriting when she types his tests. He sees himself as his own Gutenberg, a one-man publishing house.

His Macintosh becomes his integral companion. He upgrades to the 512K and later to a Mac Classic. At school, all teachers are given a Power Mac that connects to the school's network. He uses it to prepare documents, to record grades and comments for report cards, and to send and receive email internally and with parents.

His life with his beloved Macs brings not only revelations but also challenges. By the late 1990s, word processing at his school becomes the primary means for his eighth-graders to compose papers. Fewer and fewer choose to handwrite.

He agrees, however, with his colleagues, though they would not like to admit it, that they probably give better grades for word-processed papers. They look good and are often much easier to read. He sees students who use word processing develop an apparent fluency in their writing that he wishes he had when he was in school.

During a long writing assignment in which his students compose their papers in the computer lab, he discovers many of them bypassing his suggestions for revising. They simply reprint their drafts as their rewrites. Fred thinks to himself that, in this new age of word processing, they are probably not the first to find a way to avoid the task of revising.

Initially, he blames the slickness of the technology and its perfect-looking printouts. These students must believe that because their papers look good, they must be good. "Why spend time revising when my paper will not look any better, especially when Mr. Olson has lots of other work to do? Besides, Mr. Olson will probably not notice."

Well Mr. Olson notices. He realizes that he is in a new era of teaching writing, one that gives more power and control to students. They no longer wrestle with handwritten drafts, as they see their thinking emerge in sharp, clear type. They do not have to deal with yellow-lined paper with its smudges, eraser marks, and arrows that point paragraphs to different places. Instead, with clicks of the mouse they simply activate the word processor's cut and paste, spell and grammar check, fonts and font sizes, and format and style options, etc.

Fred decides to take advantage of his students' new sense of control. At the end of a writing class in the computer lab, he tells them not to print out hard copies. Instead, he has them store their word-processed drafts in a personal file that he's set up on the school's network. Before the next class, Fred assesses their drafts, inserts comments, and returns them to their files with a checkmark to indicate that he has reviewed them.

The school's default word processor is WordPerfect. He discovers its macro-key option in which he is able to preprogram words and phrases that he can use as comments to improve their drafts. He creates control + shortcut keys, so he can direct the comments into their documents. He makes his macros in a bold Helvetica font, which is in stark contrast to the Times twelve-point font that he requires them to use.

His macros include preprogrammed prompts that indicate spelling and grammar errors, the need to restructure sentences, make organizational changes, and revise content. He also inserts question marks and brackets in Helvetica around poorly written sentences and paragraphs to indicate that they should be revised. He tells students to read his comments and respond in their own voice—and then purge his notations and reformat before resubmitting their drafts or final paper.

More students revise and rewrite. They also appreciate not having to take time to print out hard copies, not having to wait for his handwritten comments the next day—*and* not having to struggle to interpret Fred's poor handwriting! Their writing becomes seamless from draft to final copy. And, the school saves lots of paper! This process means more work for them—and for Fred—but results in better papers.

Only later does Fred realize that he was tapping into a world that was becoming natural for students. He grew up in a handwriting culture and knew of colleagues who still preferred to handwrite first drafts before word processing. (Some of his present writer friends still handwrite first drafts.) He was grateful that he discovered a way to encourage students to write effectively inside the medium of word processing.

Fred's decision demonstrates that teachers must stay abreast of the culture in which their students reside. Had Fred insisted on handwritten drafts, for example, he would have been imposing a Luddite culture onto his students. More than likely, they would have complied, as most prefer to please their teachers. But, they would not have been prepared to live and work inside the world of word processing.

Learning to write remains fundamental to education. People learn to write by writing and rewriting and rewriting. Regardless of which technology they choose, the writing depends upon writers doing the work. Incorporating the power of macros allowed Fred to help students make a smooth transition into the world of word processing that includes rewriting. While perhaps not aware of it at the time, his students appreciated his efforts to integrate their word processing with his needs as a teacher. They knew they were becoming better writers.

~ ~ ~

Postscript: Twelve years later it's tablets. At the same school where Fred Olson created his macro-key solution to rewriting, the board votes to put iPads into the hands of teachers and require that students purchase them within two years. Were he still in the school, he wonders how he would respond.

He likes to think that he would be a pioneer as he had been with word processing in the computer lab. He thinks that he would look forward to creating approaches with the iPad, as he had with the computer's macro keys.

However, in the case of the iPad, being the same kind of pioneer may not be relevant. Fred recalls that around twenty years ago, when the computer appeared in classrooms, it was an intermittent tool for teachers and students. When it came time to write papers, he and his students migrated to the school's computer lab.

However some of his colleagues resisted using computers, just as years before math teachers had resisted hand-held calculators. Some colleagues did not have a computer at home, nor did some of the students. Now, because everyone will have an iPad, Fred believes that it will be instantly ubiquitous.

Fred bets that the iPads will be more collegial than computers. He can't wait to use them. Unlike having a computer in the classroom or having students write in labs, the iPad will be in everyone's hands throughout the day. Unlike texting that separates people when in one another's presence, he envisions the iPad as an interactive tool that will stimulate engaged conversations.

He imagines, too, that teachers and students will take frequent "Internet Sabbaths" away from the devices by turning them upside-down and simply deciding to engage with one another face-to-face.[3] Fred certainly hopes so.

POINTS TO PURSUE

Encounter with newness

Have you absorbed a new technology, methodology, or innovative curriculum—as Fred Olson did with his Macs—that changed your teaching? In this chapter, Fred discovers that he needs to be creative when responding to his students who use word processing. He uses his facility with the computer to develop macro keys to critique their writing.

Have you found the need to be inventive to meet the challenges that technology demands? If not, how could you learn?

Meeting students on their terms

Fred's discovery that his students take shortcuts with their writing enables him to discover a better way to teach—and more importantly, for his students to learn.

Have you struggled with the integration of technology in your classroom? Have you had to be inventive to connect with you students? Do you use an iPad? Are you prepared to respond to the next technologies soon to arrive? What can you do to stay abreast with the rush of technological culture? Why should you?

Establish a dialogue with other teachers with your ideas. Log on to Teachingthatmatters.wordpress.com and join the conversation.

THE IRREVERENT DILBERT: PROVIDE CHOICES FOR STUDENTS

Dilbert's choice to be a group of one inspires Shelley Mason, a first-grade teacher, to provide choices for her students.

Sunday's "Dilbert" opens with Pointy-Haired Boss declaring to his team,
    "We'll break into small groups to discuss options."
    "Why?" Dilbert responds, "Do you think we'll be smarter when we're in small groups?"
    After they banter back and forth about the optimum group size, Pointy-Haired Boss gives in.
    "Fine! Just break into whatever size you think makes sense."
    In the final panel, Dilbert sits alone at a conference table.
    "I like your style, Dilbert."
    "Thank you for noticing," Dilbert replies.[4]

Following in her mother's footsteps, five years ago Shelley Mason became a teacher. She considers herself somewhat traditional but open to innovative practices. A good student in college, she brought strong beliefs about teaching into her school. She loves her first-grade classroom, her twenty-seven boys and girls sitting at their four-desk clusters. Despite their restlessness at times, she sees herself teaching them well. Her students enjoy her positive attitude and her willingness to joke around with them.

When she sees Dilbert's decision in the comic to sit alone, however, it jolts her. She's never thought of separating students from their clusters, as that is the way she was taught to teach—and it seems to work most of the time. After all, she believes it is her responsibility to decide how her students should work.

Her middle school colleagues, however, prefer flexible small groups, while her high school teacher friends say they prefer to give whole group lessons, often choosing to lecture to their students sitting in rows. Shelley and many of her elementary colleagues prefer to keep their desks in fixed clusters.

Shelley is intrigued with Dilbert's choice to sit alone and do nothing. Obviously, he has no interest in improving his knowledge or contributing to the company. However, she sees his decision to sit alone as his choice. As she thinks about it, she wonders how Dilbert's action might apply to her classroom.

- Can she risk encouraging her students to make choices as to where they work?
- Can she trust if they sit alone they will want to work?
- If she chooses to provide more opportunities for how they'll work, will her students be as productive?

- And, will she still have the same control over her students?

The next morning, she notices Ryan fidgeting in his cluster.

> "This is nothing new for him," she says to herself. "Yet, today he seems particularly anxious." He persists. Exasperated with his behavior, she stops the lesson and asks, "Ryan, what's bothering you? Is there somewhere else you'd like to sit!?"
>
> He immediately points to the empty desk in the corner of the room. She takes a moment and then points to the seat. A relieved Ryan gathers up his materials and dashes over to the desk and immediately quiets down for the rest of the morning.

That evening, Shelley shares with her husband, Mitch, who's a middle school music teacher, about her decision to let Ryan sit alone. They often have active conversations about teaching.

> "You know what surprises me, Mitch. It was not so much Ryan's insistence on sitting alone at that desk as it was that none of my other students made a similar request. They continued on as usual. I wonder if some of them are uncomfortable to ask me for something for themselves. Perhaps they do what I ask just to please me. Yet, it's really curious that in my five years I see students coming to school more restless and less able to focus. Do you find that to be true in your music classes?"
>
> "Well now that you mention it, yes. Music for many kids is a stretch—and I don't have enough class time to build a strong commitment."
>
> "I wonder if the presence of cell phones is causing this restlessness. Some of my first-grade students have cell phones—and several of them have smartphones! Sometimes, their minds seem to be elsewhere.
>
> "Remember the Dilbert cartoon I showed you last Sunday? The one where Dilbert sits alone? It led me to think about the seating in my classroom. I believe it actually influenced me to ask Ryan about his restlessness.
>
> "Perhaps my insistence upon cluster seating might not be such a good idea. When I think about it, I notice that in different situations students show preferences. Peter and Sam become calm when I read aloud, while George, Mary, and Veronica fidget. When it comes to math, nearly half the group seems to disengage while the others are into it, especially Ryan.
>
> "The same type of pattern holds true for other situations. I think I could take advantage of my observations and make lessons more palatable for more students."
>
> "I think you are on to something here," Mitch says.

The next morning, Shelley sees her colleague, Judy Wilson, in the hall outside their classrooms. A veteran first-grade teacher and well-known for her imaginative methods, Judy has been a longtime favorite of parents and is willing to share ideas with colleagues. Among many of her innovations are her multiple seating patterns. Shelley asks if she might observe just how she uses them.

Once Shelley sees how Judy mixes up her seating, she returns to her classroom and immediately draws five seating arrangements on chart paper for groups from as large as five to as small as two. She can't wait to show the charts to her students—and teach them how to arrange desks quickly and efficiently.

All this excitement from one Sunday's Dilbert! From Dilbert's willingness to ask his question and then choose to sit alone. Shelley, already a confident teacher who thought that she had her ducks in a row about how to teach her fifth graders, discovers a broader palette. Dilbert's action alerts her to observe her students' preferences more closely and to pay attention to what works best for each of them.

She now realizes that she can provide different choices during class to suit the various needs of her students. She feels ready to discover other ideas to expand her repertoire for their benefit—and for her. At the same time she recognizes that she will have to maintain a balance between allowing students to make personal choices and her making choices for the whole class. A new challenge but certainly exciting!

Shelley feels that she's been released from having to do what she always has done in her first five years. She knows now that teaching can be full of surprises, that new perspectives are just around the corner. She can't wait to share her insights at the next faculty meeting.

POINTS TO PURSUE

Irreverent inspiration

Shelley Mason surprises herself with her inspiration from Dilbert's choice to sit alone. What delights one, however, is her openness to reexamine her teaching principles in search of better ways for her students to succeed.

Have you been inspired by someone or something that surprises you? Have you taken it as an inspiration and run with it as far as you could? Are you willing to reexamine what you do every day and rethink your effectiveness? It takes courage.

Ryan's fidgetiness

Soon after Shelley responds to her Dilbert inspiration, she confronts the fidgety Ryan. By asking him, "Is there somewhere else you'd like to sit?" she opens the door for him to find personal space—and opens the door for herself to discover new seating patterns for all her students.

Has a child's reaction moved you to reconsider your practice? If so, what did you do? If you find that making changes is difficult, what can you do to become more flexible? After all, changes in practice are necessary if you are to keep up with the changing nature of students and society.

Choice

Perhaps the most significant issue comes at the end of this section of the chapter: Shelley's recognition that "she will have to maintain a balance between allowing students to make personal choices and her making choices for the whole class." If you allow student choice in your teaching, how do you decide when to do it and when not to?

Establish a dialogue with other teachers with your ideas. Log on to Teachingthatmatters.wordpress.com and join the conversation.

PORTALS INTO THE LARGER WORLD: EXPAND STUDENTS' WORLDVIEWS

When Emily Hammond commits to reach beyond the classroom, she encourages her students to work harder.

How can teachers create portals for students that will connect them to the larger world? To provide them with opportunities to reach a larger audience?

Dangerous questions perhaps. On the surface, they might be interpreted as trying to emulate our celebrity-seeking culture. "Why," a teacher might ask, "encourage my students to seek a larger audience?" "Why not leave such matters to the adult world?" "If I decide to pursue this path, will I promote an *American Idol* attitude at an early age, one that teaches seeking fame as the important goal in life?"

After a long week with her fifth graders, Emily Hammond decides to see the movie *Julie and Julia*.[5] Julie Powell, who was unemployed at the time, cooks and blogs her way through Julia Child's *Mastering the Art of French Cooking*. Despite challenges and setbacks, she persists.

Her life changes when a *New York Times* reporter discovers her blog and reviews her project. The review creates a portal for Julie into a wider world well beyond her blog circle. Without it she would not have had her book published—or had a movie produced.

On her way home, Emily reflects on the movie and its possible relevance to her classroom. Having been teaching fifth grade for nearly five years, she likes discovering new ways to engage her students. She's always been like that. This year, she has a somewhat difficult group, as several of her twenty-six students are from dysfunctional families and four of them are on challenging Individual Education Plans (IEPs).

"When I think about it," Emily says to herself, "my classroom, like every classroom in my school, is a private world. I teach my children to listen to me, do seat work, take quizzes and tests, write, discuss, and produce projects. Except for the science fair, the class play, sports, and other competitions, they only produce for me. I imagine that when they were in primary school the classroom felt large and important. By now, I wonder if they might want more."

Emily wonders if schools are inherently closed institutions. Except for aides and assistants, she and her colleagues are not accustomed to having other adults in their room. Despite being publicly funded, they consider their classrooms to be their private domain.

Betty Johnson, a lifelong fifth-grade teacher in Emily's school, close to retirement, and beloved in the community, has never allowed colleagues to observe her exemplary methods. She has devoted her life to the school and has everyone's respect. But Betty believes her classroom is her domain and hers alone. Curiously, no one questions her right.

Emily wonders if Betty's example reflects the reason that teachers treat their classrooms as private and prefer not to reach out to the larger world. In a conversation one weekend with a colleague, Mike Haines, a neighbor and a sixth-grade teacher from a school across town, Emily brings up her concern.

"Mike, have you thought much about our classrooms as private domains? Have you ever thought how alone we and our kids are? Last weekend, I saw the film *Julie and Julia*, the one about Julia Child and blogger Julie Powell, and began to wonder about how isolated my classroom is. Have you ever thought about this?"

"Now that you ask, I have. Perhaps you've not heard, but recently my colleagues and I have been connecting our students via the Internet to students at a school in Finland. Just this week we had our first Skype connection in which we each shared what we'd like to have happen between us. It was very interesting. Luckily, the Finnish kids know English.

"For the past year, we have been widening the scope of our classrooms. We realize that our sixth graders live in a much wider world than we did at their age. So, we've decided to give them opportunities to connect with others.

"We've come a long way since we began this process six months ago. We first had them write letters and essays to each other instead of always writing for us. We found that more of them became involved and more imaginative. We then expanded this approach and had them write to students in other grades and even to students in other schools. Again, their writing improved—and we received interesting responses.

"So, we upped the level again and encouraged them to write letters and commentaries to newspapers and later to selected blogs. This was so successful that we decided to expand the writing process again and teach them how do research on issues that concern the community (this year we focused on stream pollution) and then how to write petitions to local government officials about their findings. This was challenging but proved to be well worth it.

"Now we are using the Internet to connect with students from Finland. It will be interesting to see how well it works."

"Wow, Mike, you have created real-life learning experiences for your students. I bet they really like what you are doing."

"Yes, they seem to."

Emily thought again about the movie. Julie's persistence to replicate Julia Child's recipes and write a blog created an audience. Unlike celebrity breakouts that result in fifteen minutes of fame, hers came from a strong work ethic. Her blog opened her to a wider network that ultimately came to the attention of the *New York Times*. It's one way that the real world works.

Emily realized, both from the movie and from her conversation with Mike, that she can inculcate new understandings for her students. She can show them how to set a goal and persist to its conclusion. She can teach them to be proud to share their learning not only with each other and their families but also through portals to other interested parties. And, she can nurture the power of a strong work ethic as Julie had as a cook and blogger.

Perhaps her classroom could create its own blog?

POINTS TO PURSUE

Balancing intimacy and portals

Emily Hammond wonders whether or not her fifth-grade classroom is "big enough." She wonders if her students might need a larger audience. After seeing the film "Julie and Julia," she begins to consider ways to extend the private world of her classroom.

Have you had similar thought about your classroom? Have you considered ways to expand its presence? Do you think it is a good idea?

The classroom as a private domain

Emily is baffled by Betty Johnson's attitude of making her classroom exclusively her own throughout her long career. Have you ever wondered about the relationship between publicly funded classrooms and teachers' claims that they are private? Do you feel your classroom is your domain? How might reframing this attitude change the way you teach?

Expanding the reach of the classroom

When teachers seek out ideas from other teachers, they discover different ways to teach. Emily's conversation with Mike Haines, who teaches in a neighboring school, opens her eyes to new ways to use writing to expand the reach of her classroom.

Have you used writing to take your students into the larger world? Has it worked well? What about creating a classroom blog?

Establish a dialogue with other teachers with your ideas. Log on to Teachingthatmatters.wordpress.com and join the conversation.

NOTES

1. See chapter 8, "Symphony: *Teach* to the Whole Child."
2. Michael Schmoker, *Results Now*, 58–75.
3. This concept for Sabbaths was coined by William Powers, *Hamlet's Blackberry*, chapter 13: "Disconnectopia: The Internet Sabbath." See further discussion of disconnecting in chapter 7, "Sabbaths: Take Occasions toTurn Off Electronic Devices."
4. "Dilbert," *Boston Globe*, August 15, 2010.
5. *Julie and Julia* (Columbia Pictures, 2009).

ELEVEN
Beyond the Classroom

These four essays from sources beyond the classroom encourage teachers to implement alternative approaches.

AT THE CENTER: VIEW THE INTERNET AS A METAPHOR FOR THE UNIVERSE

When Mark Norris understands that the Internet is an expression of the universe, it lets him know that we reside at the center.

Wherever you are is the entry point. —Kabir

During his forty years in the classroom, teaching became a process of discovery for Mark Norris. In his final year of teaching middle school, the spring of 1999, he wrote the following essay that he entitled "At the Center."

> The Internet is the first global community. Any person of any age, race, ethnic group, location, status, wealth, class, height, weight, and intelligence can participate. Young children, teenagers, parents, executives, artists, and seniors. No credentials necessary. No one in charge. The Internet has no boss.
>
> Any site is a click or two away. Sequencing is personal. The magic of hyperlinks allows people to create unique pathways. Like the brain's synapses, the Internet leaps almost at will often taking the user to unimagined places that are as full of possibilities as they are empty with improbabilities. Instant messaging and shared-screen interactivity opens the power of web collaboration. Given the whole-is-larger-than-the-sum-of-its-parts paradigm, who knows where this might lead.
>
> When logging on, we enter at the center and become immersed. The Net has no beginning and no end. No matter how long we migrate, no

matter how far we navigate, we remain at the center. We never reach the edge. We can be anywhere from where we are. It is like our imagination, except that it moves by a mouse rather than by thoughts.

As physical beings, we function in beginnings, middles, and ends. Surfing the Internet invites us to think otherwise; we soon realize that we remain at the center no matter how long or how far we navigate. Whenever our access is restricted or interrupted, we lose contact with its freedom and flow. So it is in life, we realize that freedom of choice is essential if we are to fulfill our potential.

Metaphysically, we are born at the center. At any point in our lives—as in the universe—we are at the center. Yet, we mark our years with holidays, birthdays, anniversaries, vacations, and report cards. We define time by hours, minutes, and seconds. We live by days, nights, weeks, months, and years. We create separate places. We attempt to make life secure by our identities, age, position, and status. Sometimes, we try to hold on to them, especially our youth. When we understand, however, that we are always at the center, perhaps we will stop trying to be somewhere else.

The arrival of the Internet may be our way of realizing that we are all accounted for, that we all are together at the center. The Internet belongs to all of us. We all have access to all there is. We can participate if we choose. I have seen the Internet and it is us.

Despite advances, since his essay, on how to access the Internet—specifically Google's search engines—Mark understands that we remain at the center. No doubt further changes lie ahead. Perhaps an Internet boss, or bosses, will take control, as they have in China. Mark certainly hopes not.

Ironically, unbeknownst to him at the time, Mark's new thinking about the universe and the Internet conditioned him to accept the head of school's sudden order that he drop teaching Russian and Chinese history in the eighth grade. It was a course he dearly loved to teach. The head of school demanded that he teach ancient history instead as a precursor to ninth-grade Western civilization, which included using the head's prescribed textbook.

Faced with this edict, Mark decided to begin his new course at the big bang. Part of his motivation was a protest against being directed as to what to teach—and that he disdained having to use the dreaded textbook. Besides, he had become intrigued with the possibility of investigating the origin of the universe with students.

Having been a longtime Carl Sagan aficionado, he rekindled his interest in this topic in conversations with Winslow Morris, Art Department head at the school. Winslow's connection at that time with the antiwar organization "Beyond War" gave him access to new thinking about the planet, the universe, and cosmology. He introduced Mark to the seminal work of Brian Swimme and Thomas Berry and shared a wide range of materials that Mark thought would be suitable for his eighth graders.

Thus, when the head of school imposed his will, Mark saw it as an opportunity to extend his love of all things Sagan and include the new thinking that Winslow had shared. Besides, if Mark began his ancient history course at Mesopotamia, he reasoned, humans would have already established government, economics, religion, social structure, and writing.

Instead, he wanted his students to delight in the origins of the universe up to the evolution of planet earth and the arrival of the first humans—and from there to the first civilizations. He intended to stake his claim to the course and resist the dreaded textbook for as long as possible.

The choice to begin with the big bang proved exhilarating. Of all the concepts that Mark and his students explored, two of them provoked considerable controversy. One was that humans are made up of atoms, as is everything in the universe, and therefore we are—each of us—99 percent empty. In fact, the universe *is* 99 percent empty, which is likely true for dark energy and dark matter as well. The conversations were sparkling.

The second idea, nearly as provocative, was the concept of the omnicentric universe, (i.e., there may not be one center around which the universe revolves). Edward Hubble saw this actuality through his telescope in 1929 when he observed that galaxies expanded away from each other in all directions. Hence, some seventy years later, Mark pondered with his students that we may be, each of us, "at the center" as evidenced by the Internet.

Later, Mark took the concepts of 99 percent emptiness and omnicentricity and linked them to the wisdom of Confucius, Lao Tzu, and Buddha that he loved to teach in his Chinese history course. Despite the intricacies of these teachings, his students gleaned worthwhile insights that they indicated in conversations and in their essays.

Knowing that adolescents usually see the world from their "center," Mark was pleased that many of them began to understand the earth and Milky Way Galaxy's omnicentric presence in the universe. Fewer seemed able to grasp that humans are 99 percent empty. That was a tough one. And, he decided not to attempt to give tests, as he realized that any questions he posed would be open to speculation and thus difficult to grade.

Mark framed the human-history part of the course around Bill McKibben's concept of footprints.[1] In the first week of school, he wrote a two-page letter addressed to his students and their parents in which the opening paragraph was, "Footprints. It's all about footprints." He concluded:

> Given the exponential growth of the human presence, we live in a world that demands our full attention in order to survive. The ancients provided us with the power to create and savor as well as the power to

dominate and destroy. We need to study them to learn how we came to create such large footprints. We need also to learn their wisdom, a wisdom that can deepen and enlighten our consciousness and help us succeed on our planet. We are about to embark upon a wonderful adventure together—in class and hopefully on the earth in this special time in which we live.

Enjoy the ride.

~ ~ ~

Nearly twenty years earlier at a lecture at Dartmouth College, Mark heard Carl Sagan share his exhilarating view of the origin of the universe. It was at the time of Sagan's first broadcast of the *Cosmos* television series. His claim that "we are made of star stuff" still lingers deep in Mark's mind.

After reading *The Dragons of Eden, Shadows of Our Forgotten Ancestors,* and *Contact,* Mark became a fierce advocate of Sagan's cosmological thinking.[2] Sagan set him on a path that drew him into the omnicentric universe and later into the omnicentric Internet.

When Mark looks back on his ancient history course, he realizes that the head of school's directive (without any input from Mark) that he teach ancient history gave him a silver lining. With the support of Winslow Morris's resources, he designed an original and exciting path for his students to learn about the ancients, one he never would have created had he continued to teach his Russian and Chinese history course.

Mark wishes he could say that his approach to his ancient history course was a collaborative effort between him and his History Department colleagues, but alas it was his own journey. It confirms one of the arguments presented in this book that the impetus to change can come from multiple sources. Mark now realizes how lucky he was to have had this adventure that resulted from such an unlikely circumstance.

Once teachers understand that they live "at the center," they will feel empowered and humbled at the same time. So will their students. Together, they can connect with the universe perspective from its beginnings and view planet earth in a new and exciting way. They may be able to put present-day problems into a longer term outlook and see potential for new solutions.

Humans, after all, have come this far and have invented wondrous things. It is not inevitable that humans will fail—or fail to evolve—before the sun dies. Optimism helps to make a positive future reality possible. It certainly puts a plus on the life force.

POINTS TO PURSUE

Include the universe perspective

How powerful to think of the Internet as an extended human brain, as a metaphor for the universe. If we humans are always at the center, perhaps it will free us to become less linear and more ambiguous, more willing to meander, rather than to plunge straight ahead. It may open you as teachers to be more present with students, rather than acting as if you have to take them somewhere. What do you think?

Trust teachers to decide

With the hierarchical structure of schools still in place, teachers are often given little latitude in deciding what to teach and how. The example in this chapter, however, depicts a teacher who, despite orders from his head of school, takes nearly total control of his curriculum.

Do you think that if teachers were to have more control on what and how to teach, classroom learning would improve? Or are standards and accountability necessary to ensure that something is taught? Is there a middle ground? What do you think?

Establish a dialogue with other teachers with your ideas. Log on to Teachingthatmatters.wordpress.com and join the conversation.

BYSTANDER: CHOOSE NONACTION IN TIMES OF STRESS

In responding to frenetic moments in the classroom, an old man's nonaction reveals the strength of standing still.

Bystanders wait.

In a world seeking fifteen minutes of fame, a bystander's nonaction may appear to be nonsense. In the rush to success, we prefer to be proactive. If we choose to sit and contemplate, we might feel we will miss opportunities—or perceived opportunities.

When we lose our keys, we rush around and try to find them, rather than sit still and let our mind recall where they are. We ride the merry-go-round in anticipation of reaching the gold ring, rather than choosing to take pleasure in riding the merry-go-round to ride the merry-go-round.

Elissa Ely reminds us of the bystander. In a brief essay, she describes a reality cooking show in which chefs compete in teams. During the relay segment, each chef was allowed ten minutes to work the recipe before the next chef, who was blindfolded, had to figure out what to do. Their energy was frenetic, except for one older man who appeared immobile in front of his frying pan. Ely writes:

> Gladiators ran past while he stood in his apron. After about a minute of stillness, his face started to glow with a look of comprehension. He understood what he needed to do. Newton's apple had fallen, and he was in position to receive it. Now, he was ready to cook it.[3]

How often during a lesson do we as teachers choose nonaction? When do we recognize that we simply can stop to contemplate, rather than to hurry on to the next thing? When do we ask for or allow students to take time for nonaction? To simply be present? Or, in Ely's metaphor, to be open to "when and where the apple will drop"?

Meditation reminds us to take time to simply be. To choose nonaction. Choose to wait and become receptive, spontaneous, and open. Only then do we see what we need and allow it to come to us. We emulate the Taoist, Winnie the Pooh, his uncanny ability to be in accord with the way things as they are—*wu wei*, do without doing—like water that flows unimpeded on a path of least resistance.[4]

Sometimes a teacher finds herself in a flurry. Everything seems to come at her all at once. Everyone around her acts like Ely's gladiator chefs. She feels compelled to figure a way out before she is consumed. She senses she has no control.

At such moments, she would do well to invoke firefighter Norman McLean's decision to stand still in the face of an oncoming raging forest fire. Instead of seeking a way to flee, McLean starts to burn the grass around him so as to deny the fire fuel. Thirteen of his men think he is crazy and flee on a path that appears open to cliffs nearby. They all die but MacLean and one other survives.[5]

As teachers, we can choose not to flee when students press us, when events take over. We stand still and assess what's happening. We allow others to see where they are and what they are doing. We trust the trees in the forest to know where we are.[6] We allow the onslaught to retreat. We deprive it of its fuel. We create a Norman McLean reprieve to give students time to choose to come back to us.

Ely's old man won the competition, much to the envy of the other frenetic chefs. She writes, "Speed under stress is considered a form of mastery, but slowing down—resisting instinct, drive, and all biology—is gladiatorial."

In the "race to the top," in feverish attention to tests, schools threaten to deny students the joy of being, of self-discovery, of inventive curiosity. When the bewildering concerns of a confused adult world toss us about, we do not need to breed that confusion in students.

As teachers, we can trust deep understanding and choose to curtail this downward spiraling and instead open students to the joys of learning. Learning that drops in. Learning from each other. From the world. From inside. From nonaction.

POINTS TO PURSUE

Stand still and wait until the mud settles

In a busy, rush-rush world, how delightful are those moments when teachers choose to be still—and help students to be still as well. Just being, counterintuitive to our get-ahead culture, an important lesson for all.

How can you make this happen? How can you help students become patient before acting? Perhaps you could have them stand quietly for two minutes. Simply stand. Why would you?

"Race to the Top," a race to nowhere?

Do you agree with the first sentence of the last paragraph: "In the 'race to the top,' in feverish attention to tests, schools threaten to deny students the joy of being, of self-discovery, of inventive curiosity."

Is the path to test scores scaring teachers and students? Or are these tests necessary in our global world? Compare the Finnish and South Korean education systems before you decide. When you decide, act on your conviction.

Establish a dialogue with other teachers with your ideas. Log on to Teachingthatmatters.wordpress.com and join the conversation.

IGNITION KEY: OBSERVE WHAT'S IN FRONT OF YOU

Phil Rogers makes good choices when he pays close attention to what's in front of him.

On his way to present another workshop for new teachers at a nearby charter school, Phil Rodgers parks his car in front of his local market to refill his coffee mug. He returns to his car and discovers that his key does not fit into the ignition. No matter how many times he tries, it only goes in part way. "Something's wrong with the ignition," he says to himself.

Phil knows that he needs to be at his workshop soon, so he jumps out of the car and returns to the market. He tells Rob, the congenial proprietor, about his predicament (and that his car is stuck in a loading zone!). Rob immediately offers his car. "At least," Phil says to himself, "I will get to the workshop."

Thinking that he might not have the right key, he decides to return to his condo a block away to retrieve a second set of keys. About halfway up the street Phil discovers that he is holding the key to his wife's car. Shortly before he stopped for coffee, he had taken her car from the garage to her studio, as she was hobbled by a broken toe. Inadvertently, he put her key into the pocket with his key.

"Why," Phil asks himself, did I first assume that the ignition was defective, and not that I might have had the wrong key? Why at that moment didn't I stop to assess other possibilities? All I needed to do was to check my pockets, and I would have found the right key!"

Just that morning, he had read a piece on the Internet about paying attention that recalled Buddhist monk Thich Nhat Hanh's concept of "wash the dishes to wash the dishes." Hanh's admonition reminded him to pay attention to what's in front of him. Had Phil done so with the key, he would have seen that he taken out his wife's key from his pocket instead of his own.

Yet, when he has a chance to act, in this case "to put the key in the ignition to put the key in the ignition," Phil allows his mind immediately to assume that he knows what the problem is. "I wonder how often in pressure situations I ignore Hanh's wisdom? How often do I think that I understand before I take time to look and listen? How often do I really pay attention to what's in front of me?"

He wonders if he is a victim of his own "think-I-know-best" mind when confronted with problems, like his desire to force the wrong key in the ignition? He remembers that he had grown up in a culture that taught him to "know because I know" first and ask questions later.

John Robinson recalls that twenty-years ago he could not wait to be a teacher. He barely had enough patience to complete his master's program, as he was eager to have his own classroom. After several interviews, he signs a contract to teach high school European and Asian history in a small college town, just what he wanted.

From his first day in front of his students, they find him to be energetic, funny, and knowledgeable. His lessons often become animated. He is not afraid to ask provocative questions. Many of his assignments are creative, such as his Spanish Armada interactive map assignment.

As is true for many of his first-year colleagues, John is confident that he'll like his students, and they will like him. Given that most of them enter his classroom with a smile and friendly exchanges, he believes that he is on the right path.

> Five years later, John sees Helen Shaw, a former student from his first year, at a drugstore counter. He remembers her as one of his more attentive students, though somewhat quiet and reticent to speak in class. In the course of their conversation, Helen drops what for him is a bomb.
>
> "Mr. Robinson, "I think that you believed that boys were smarter than girls. I remember that my friends and I often received C's on our papers while the same few boys always got A's."
>
> "You mean, Helen, you really thought that I favored boys?"
>
> "Well, yes," Helen replied shyly.
>
> John is taken aback. "Thinking that one sex is smarter than the other," he says to himself, "That's not good." From that day, John is determined to stay open to each of his students' potential every day in his class.

Later in the week, John comes across Thich Nhat Hanh's *The Miracle of Mindfulness*. He's immediately struck by the opening incident in the book in which Hanh's friend Allen recounts his discovery of not dividing his time into parts but instead seeing whatever he does as his own time. A couple of pages later, Hanh challenges another friend, Jim, on how to wash the dishes. "There are two ways to wash the dishes," Hanh says. "The first is to wash the dishes to have clean dishes and the second is to wash the dishes to wash the dishes."[7]

Upon reading this exchange, a light bulb lights up in John's head. "Of course, pay attention to what's in front of me *without* assumptions, *without* judgment!" Yet, he knows that the demands from having more than one hundred students every day makes it doubly challenging to see each one as he or she is on any given day. Still, John becomes more determined to see his students as they are, not as he thinks they should be.

"I know just how I will begin," he says to himself. "Why not grade student papers without their names? Because all of them word process, I will not know whose paper I am reading. I think that will be fair. I can't wait to see Helen and thank her for her candid comment!"

~ ~ ~

Three hours later, after his incident with the ignition keys, Phil Rodgers closes his teacher workshop with his story. He has just led a discussion on ways for teachers to help students learn to take responsibility for their behavior. He encourages them not to make quick assumptions when students go off track. "When possible," he says, "pay attention, listen, and wait to see all the possibilities before you decide, before you act."

He knows he is speaking to himself as well.

POINTS TO PURSUE

Be present, be aware

In the rush-rush of modern life, we often steam ahead before we know where we are. We move to the next thing without paying attention to what's actually in front of us. In the ignition-key incident, Phil Rodgers acted ahead of what he could easily have known. No doubt, had he sat in his car with Thich Nhat Hanh's "to wash the dishes to wash the dishes" mindset, he would have seen that he indeed had the wrong keys in his hand.

How can you, in the rush-rush of the school day, develop Thich Nhat Hanh's mantra—*and* get everything done?

See students as they are

Helen Shaw tells her former teacher, John Robinson, that he prejudges students. Considering himself a good teacher, he becomes determined from that moment to not make assumptions about his students. Do you decide quickly which students are better than others? If so, what are willing to do about it?

Thich Nhat Hanh's "wash the dishes to wash the dishes" mantra, alerts John to stay in the present and extend his thinking. He decides to grade student papers without names. What do you think of this idea? What would happen to your relationship with students if you decided to try this practice?

Establish a dialogue with other teachers with your ideas. Log on to Teachingthatmatters.wordpress.com and join the conversation.

Chapter 11

PAPER CUTTER: MAKE PLANS BUT KNOW YOUR INTENTIONS

When Brett Cranbrook becomes flexible with his plans, he is able to keep his intentions.

One mid-afternoon, Brett Cranbrook suddenly remembers that he promised his local bank that he would bring display materials for his new book. Maria, the congenial branch manager, reserved the lobby table for him that she makes available every month to customers who want to share their ideas or offer services.

Brett quickly prints a comment sheet from early readers of his book; locates a canvas bag in which he puts in a copy of the book, a book stand, business cards, and photos. He leaves in a hurry, as he plans to stop by his wife's print studio on the way to use her paper cutter to make a clean border for the comment sheet.

When he arrives at the studio, his wife says that he cannot use the paper cutter, because a printmaker is renting her press. She offers to get a matte knife and trim the paper, a method she prefers to using the paper cutter.

Brett fusses. He planned, after all, to use her paper cutter. He already dissed the idea at home of using a ruler to set margins because he knows that he would not cut straight lines with scissors. Instead, he makes a plan to use her paper cutter. Had his intention been to have his paper trimmed, he might have quickly accepted her offer. But he's stuck on his plan to use her paper cutter. He fusses again.

His wife trims the paper with her matte knife.

Brett awakes the next morning, with three words in his mind: *intention, plan,* and *paper cutter.* He immediately recognizes that he still needs to learn a lesson about something that has provoked him for years. If he had gathered the display materials for the bank with the *intention* to trim the comment sheet, he would have been open as to how it would have been done. Instead, he put a specific *plan* in his mind—to use his wife's *paper cutter.*

As a middle school social studies teacher, now for nearly ten years, Brett has been open to new approaches to improve his teaching. He cannot remember a year without his taking a course or attending extended workshops. He wants to learn all he can about teaching.

At an Understanding by Design workshop, Brett discovers the importance of the three principles of Backward Design: setting *desired results* at every level from lessons to courses; being clear as to *evidence* that indicates that learning has taken place; and *planning* well-defined lessons, units, and courses.

He's always thought that planning is important. Good teachers plan lessons and establish clear intentions for all aspects of a unit or a course—and know full well what they want students to know by the end of the year. It's unfair, Brett thinks, to lead students down a road that they cannot see.

Yet he knows that lesson plans, well intentioned as they may be, may not serve well when the unexpected happens. At such moments, he realizes that he has a choice: to either roll with the unexpected to see where it might take him and his students or to try to stick to his original plan.

In his earlier years, he tended to resist changing his plans even when he knew that they were not working. Now he's become more open to student responses, except when he senses they are deliberately trying to take him off track. He discovers that unexpected input from students often helps to move his classes toward important understandings—usually not far from his intentions. It's taken him time to trust and allow this process to unfold.

In his personal life, however, Brett finds this approach more challenging. Whenever he decides what he wants or needs to do, he expects it to go according to *his* plan. A simple task, like using his wife's paper cutter, he thinks ought to happen without a hitch. Except this kind of planning only takes him into account. He's not prepared for a glitch. He does not have any students in the room to put him in check.

As Brett looks back on this incident with his wife, he realizes that in the months before he has been offered wisdom to cope with such matters. In a conversation with a new colleague, Christina Ward, he shared his concern about his impatience, especially when things did not go his way. Christina told him about the *I Ching* and how it helped her stay in the present and be in accord with the way things are. He decided to consult it several times a week. He found that reading the *I Ching* was beginning to make sense.

Still, in the case of the paper cutter incident, Brett realizes that he failed to heed the *I Ching*'s advice not to resist. So the next morning he asks the *I Ching*: "How can I remain unstructured when making plans?" After casting the three special coins that Christina gave him, Hexagram 23 "Po/Splitting Apart" appeared. Of all three commentaries, Carol Anthony's makes the most sense: "When our attitude becomes correct, a change in conditions is brought about, much as when a shoal of fishes changes direction in unison. . . . Acceptance leads to success." [8]

Brett interprets her words to mean that he will find peace of mind in his personal life when he stays with his *intentions* rather than trying to enforce his *plans*. And, as an unexpected dividend, he will also be helpful to others (his wife will appreciate that!). Brett imagines, as well, how valuable this advice is for teachers who face challenges every day when trying to fulfill their plans.

Perhaps, Brett wonders, people may take from the *I Ching* only what they want to. Yet, it's uncanny how often it speaks to what he seeks to know. In this instance, it also tells him to keep on his inner path, to move on, and to realize that he can learn how to remain open and unstructured.

Brett welcomes these words, but he knows that he will be confronted again with the decision of either fulfilling his intentions or enforcing his plans. He knows that it won't be about a paper cutter, but perhaps he'll be better prepared.

POINTS TO PURSUE

Know the difference between plans and outcomes

Lesson plans can be a teacher's best friend, but only when they are framed inside broader intentions. How can you make wise plans that enable you to become flexible after you involve students?

How will you survive—and teach well—when students disrupt your plans? When do you resist? And when can you trust the flow that will take you and your students where you truly need to go?

Seeking wisdom

Life—in particular the teaching life—can be filled with disruptions, instant challenges, and unanticipated difficulties. How have you coped? Where do you seek inner quiet? Where do you find sources that bring you the perspective that allows you to step back, let go, and accept what is?

How might the *I Ching*, Buddhist sutras, Hebrew Psalms, Christian teachings, and other spiritual paths provide solace for you in difficult times? Have you chosen a path to guide you?

Establish a dialogue with other teachers with your ideas. Log on to Teachingthatmatters.wordpress.com and join the conversation.

NOTES

1. Bill McKibben, "A Special Moment in History" (*Atlantic Monthly*, May 1998).
2. Carl Sagan, *The Dragons of Eden: Speculations on the Evolution of Human Intelligence* (New York: Ballantine Books, 1977). Carl Sagan and Ann Druyan, *Shadows of Forgotten Ancestors: A Search for Who We Are* (New York: Ballantine Books, 1992). Carl Sagan, *Cosmos* (Random House, 1980).
3. Elissa Ely, "Slow Down and Take It All In," *Boston Globe*, May 30, 2010.
4. Benjamin Hoff, *The Tao of Pooh* (New York: E. P. Dutton, 1982).
5. With thanks to Barbara Merritt for first sharing this story with me, a story from the folk song "Cold Missouri River." The real survivor was R. Wagner Dodge as told by Norman Maclean, *Young Men and Fire*. Chicago: University of Chicago Press, 1992.
6. I first learned of this story from John Kabat-Zinn in his talk at Bancroft School, May 1999.
7. Thich Nhat Hanh, *The Miracle of Mindfulness: A Manual on Meditation* (Beacon Press, Revised Edition, 1987), 1–3.

8. Carol Anthony, *A Guide to the I Ching*, Third Edition (Stowe, MA: Anthony Publishing, Revised and Enlarged, 1988), 112.

III

See Things as They Are

Be the change you wish to see in the world. —Gandhi

When teachers and administrators understand that no practice is sacred, they assess them for what they are and become open to make changes for the better.

Part III discusses three such examples.

Schools are worlds unto themselves. They create their own realities. Administrators set up class schedules, require dress codes or uniforms, establish specific rules and regulations, including bathroom and library passes, and arrange afterschool detentions. Teachers assign seats, establish how and when to raise hands, when to go to the bathroom, how to do homework, and even where to put names and dates on papers and tests. Because expectations vary from class to class, students become confused.

Our culture is no different. Tabloids, sound bites, talk radio, and cable television create their own realities. If teachers are to teach truth to power, "to speak out to those in authority,"[1] if they are to help students understand what is real, they establish meaningful worlds in their classrooms. When necessary, they show students when "the emperor is not wearing any clothes."

"But he's not wearing anything at all!" says the child. Such is the perspective offered in the first chapter in this section on PowerPoint, Microsoft's ubiquitous software that has become a cultural meme. From its inception, PowerPoint has been hailed as an exemplary form of communication. In fact, it rarely communicates, as this chapter demonstrates. Teachers who use PowerPoint need to understand the PowerPoint emperor for who he is.

The second chapter explores our culture that rushes past before anyone has time to notice. Schools are caught up in races to nowhere, as teachers and students chase one fact, one date, one algorithm, one synonym, one score after another in hopes of beating the tests. No time to ponder. No time to wonder. No time to ruminate. Never time to do anything at its own speed.

The third chapter invites readers to step back from the ubiquitous appeals of corporations—Coca Cola, Pepsi, Ford, GE, Cialis, T-Mobile, AT&T, NFL, ABC, Citibank, Disney,[2] et al. Corporate messages appear everywhere: on television, radio, highways, roads, streets, the Internet—and in newspapers, magazines, and malls. Seven corporations control 70 percent of all media.[3]

This chapter offers a respite from this noisy culture, an opportunity to pay attention to the wisdom of a mystic who can bring solace away from the interminable pandering and attempts at mind control. The Four Agreements provides such a path.

These chapters illustrate three ways for teachers and principals to improve practice. Together they provide a model for paying attention to reality and making changes when necessary. Schools improve when the administration and faculty make decisions together to expand the greater good. They will then be the change they wish to see in their schools. They will support the dreams of their students.

NOTES

1. http://www.urbandictionary.com/define.php?term=speak%20truth%20to%20power.

2. To see a brilliant spoof of Disney's hold on the imagination of young girls, go to David Trumble's "David's Disney Princessified 'World of Women'" at http://www.womenyoushouldknow.net/flatten-heroine-artist-puts-disney-princess-filter-10-real-life-female-role-models/ (for example, Trumble changed Princess Anne Frank, "Holocaust Princess," to Anne Frank, "Diary Princess.").

3. Jerry Mander on YouTube: http://www.youtube.com/watch?v=Y_ptn-cNBJA.

TWELVE

Purge PowerPoint: See the Emperor Without His Clothes

When teachers pay attention to the ineffectiveness of PowerPoint, they discover that the emperor is not wearing any clothes.

It is March 2000. As a new consultant, Rob Tristan considers using Microsoft's PowerPoint for his teacher workshops. He wants to be an innovative presenter. As a longtime science teacher, he brought intelligence and levity to his students and colleagues.

When he consulted for a small computer firm the year before, he became a teacher of teachers; he learned how to use PowerPoint's readymade templates. He thinks that if he were to use them in his workshops, he would be showing teachers a way to improve instruction.

Rob imagines that Microsoft's slideware would jazz up his presentations and stimulate interactive participation. Instead, halfway through his first workshop, he finds that everyone's thinking is becoming constricted. Whenever he clicks to a new slide, it captures their attention and redirects the discussion. He tries using slides in another workshop and becomes convinced that participants are driven more by the sequence of the slides than by the threads of their conversations.

He sees, however, that many of his fellow consultants are still using overheads. When he co-presents with a veteran consultant at a mentor workshop for ninety teachers, she brings at least two hundred acetates that she has stuffed into a broken-down box on the floor. Yet, she is always able to find the one she wants at the moment she needs it. Her overheads appear to add to her presentation. They seem to flow better that the slideware that he tried.

So Rob surmises that he should try overheads. He makes sets of acetates that fill several binders. The more he projects them at workshops, however, the more he realizes that participants want printed copies. He also observes that some people in the room cannot see the projections well.

After several workshops, he realizes that he does not need the overheads. Instead, he decides to put what he would have shown as overheads into the printed packets. When it comes time to discuss what he would have used as an overhead, he simply opens to the page in the packet and holds it above his head as "my overhead." Participants chuckle, but it works every time; everyone focuses on that page.

Later, he realizes that he is moving in a different direction from some of his colleagues who are replacing overheads with flash drives for laptops that project PowerPoint slides (or Keynote slides, Apple's version). He opts not to try this approach again and, instead, decides to invigorate face-to-face interactions among participants.

Rob wants to counteract the encroaching digitalized culture in which people tend to pay less attention to each other and more attention to digital devices. He wants to leave constant connectivity behind. He wants his people to immerse themselves in uninterrupted listening, conversation, and reflection. He hopes that they will replicate similar practices in their classrooms.

When presenters choose to use slides as the focus of their workshops, Rob believes that they send the message—unintended perhaps—that they are *deliverers* and the participants are *recipients*. He feels that choosing not to use slides underscores his role as a facilitator. He posts an agenda and states the intended outcomes of the workshop on a whiteboard or chart paper. He repeats these outcomes in the front of carefully prepared printed packets that include graphics, provocations, ideas, jigsaw articles, readings, etc.

Throughout the day, like his colleagues, he models best practices. Participants meet in a whole group, in smaller groups, or in triads or pairs and write on their own. He emphasizes the importance of making the classroom compatible for every kind of learner, from the most sociable to the most reticent. Together they view video clips, produce different products, and take time for personal reflections. If for some reason a workshop takes a surprising turn, Rob flows with it as long it remains within the bounds of his contract.

However, he thinks that when consultants choose to act as presenters first—to use PowerPoint slideware—they establish a different dynamic. When they make the projection screen their focus, the potential for interaction becomes diminished. The presenter chooses when to project the slides. Participants often have to shift their attention back and forth from slide to presenter, from slide to presenter—and can become confused when the presenter utters different words from those on the slide.

Rob begins to wonder about the implications of PowerPoint's ubiquitous presence.

Not long after Rob ends his experiments with readymade PowerPoint slides, he discovers Edward Tufte's website. Upon reading Tufte's rampage against the misuse and overuse of PowerPoint, Rob decides to order Tufte's *The Cognitive Style of PowerPoint*.[1] In twenty-seven cogent pages, Tufte demonstrates how PowerPoint's preoccupation with style

- makes for low-resolution slides, at most about forty words on each;
- dumbs down content to fit its limited template formats;
- uses mindless, unrelated bullets;
- fails to provide narrative; and
- does all of it in "an attitude of commercialism that turns everything into a sales pitch."[2]

In *The Cognitive Style of PowerPoint* Tufte provides clear examples of the shortcomings of PowerPoint. He recounts how slides contributed to the failure to avert the Columbia space shuttle disaster; how Peter Novig's supercilious slides of the Gettysburg address diminish its impact; and how medical slides, despite their intention, fail to show cancer survival rates. In these and other examples Tufte makes clear that PowerPoint fails to deliver what it promises.

Rob particularly likes Tufte's recommendation that speakers provide a summary of their key ideas on an eleven-by-seventeen-inch paper folded in half to make four pages. He's noticed that the better he prepares his packets, the more impact they have. Tufte notes: "Thoughtfully planned handouts at your talks tell the audience that you are serious and precise; that you seek to leave traces and have consequences. And that you respect your audience."[3]

James Carroll, *Boston Globe* columnist, provides another example of the limitations of PowerPoint. He writes:

> The ubiquitous use of PowerPoint slides in military briefings about Afghanistan and Iraq has been tagged as a problem. Breaking down battle reports into bullets and bites, as Brigadier General H.R. McMaster told the *New York Times*, "can create the illusion of understanding and the illusion of control." . . . The sound-bite reduces experience to episodes shorn of context, when understanding what matters requires a honed feel precisely for the connection between episodes.[4]

Steve Jobs also loathed PowerPoint. After he returned to Apple in 1997, he demanded that product review teams not use it. He later recalled,

> I hate the way people use slide presentations instead of thinking. . . . People would confront problems by creating a presentation. I wanted them to engage, to hash things out at the tables, rather than show a

bunch of slides. People who know what they're talking about don't need PowerPoint.[5]

Yet, there are exceptions. Rob has seen a few teachers use excellent visual-based slides as focal points for discussion. He also discovered Hans Rosling's TED talks that demonstrate how PowerPoint can enhance thinking and understanding.

In his powerful talks on insights into poverty, Rosling creates slides in which colored bubbles representing countries move up on the screen and change size through time. His images are riveting, as riveting as his information. No templates, no random bullets, no pretty borders. His presentation and animated voice enraptures his audience.[6]

"Yet," Rob wonders, "How often do teachers who rely on PowerPoint slides really understand what they are projecting?" Is Steve Jobs right? Are slides used as a substitute for thinking? Or, can they encourage thinking, as Rosling ably demonstrates? Is Apple's Keynote a better option?

~ ~ ~

When teachers or presenters do not make PowerPoint slideware the focus of attention, anyone can become the center of attention. Participants can then become immersed in undistracted conversations. They observe, listen, and learn from one another. A collective wisdom emerges. They avoid, in Tufte's words, "playing around with Phluff [his term for PowerPoint content] rather than providing information, *PowerPoint allows speakers to pretend that they are giving a real talk, and audience to pretend they are listening.*"[7]

By choosing not to use PowerPoint's template slideware, teachers avoid the predicament that Soviet students in the mid-1980s said about their schooling: "Our teachers pretend to teach and we pretend to learn." It was their version of a common Soviet adage: "We pretend to work and they pretend to pay us."

Given that 10^{10} to 10^{11} PowerPoint slides are made each year,[8] perhaps massive pretending is happening right under our noses and we don't even know it!

POINTS TO PURSUE

Assess your use of PowerPoint

Rob Tristan, the consultant in this chapter, faces the same dilemmas as anyone who teaches or presents. As you reflect on his decisions, where are you on the continuum between using older technologies, like overheads, or newer ones, like PowerPoint?

As a student, did you experience endless filmstrips or overheads that taught you hardly anything? What technologies do you use to support your teaching? How do your students respond?

If you use PowerPoint, what's been your experience? As a student? As a teacher? As a presenter? What's your honest assessment as to its effects? Have you ever observed a colleague who uses PowerPoint for his presentations? What have you noticed about him and his students? What have you done about your findings?

Presenter or teacher?

As you assess your classroom (or your school, as a principal), do you see yourself as a presenter or a facilitator? Do you tell rather than teach? Is your classroom structure similar to Rob's structure for his workshops: interactive and personal and using best practices and multiple methodologies directed at different learners? How engaged are your students both in class and throughout your school?

Edward Tufte, you, and PowerPoint

What is your reaction to Edward Tufte's analysis of PowerPoint? If you could speak with him, what questions would you ask him? Visit his website, www.edwardtufte.com, for books, posters, sculpture, fine art, and where to attend his highly praised one-day course. Order *The Cognitive Style of PowerPoint: Pitching Out Corrupts Within* (Second Edition). You will not be disappointed.

Printed page versus PowerPoint

Tufte brings up a profound point: Do you agree with him that "a summary of [a presenter's] key ideas on an eleven-by-seventeen-inch paper folded in half to make four pages" holds more potential for learning than a PowerPoint presentation?

When you reflect about PowerPoint, how does Tufte's conclusion resonate with you: "*PowerPoint allows speakers to pretend that they are giving a real talk, and audience to pretend they are listening*" (italics are his).

Or do you think that Tufte's advocating four-page handouts is the argument of a reactionary practitioner in the digital age?

Hans Rosling at TED

For a brilliant use of PowerPoint, consider Google Hans Rosling at TED (www.ted.com). Rosling's sophisticated use of PowerPoint slideware demonstrates how it can enhance thinking and understanding. His slides (if you can call them that) reveal his mind to viewers. Truly an extraordinary experience.

Establish a dialogue with other teachers with your ideas. Log on to Teachingthatmatters.wordpress.com and join the conversation.

NOTES

1. Edward Tufte, *The Cognitive Style of PowerPoint* (Graphics Press, September 2003; now in its second edition, 2006).
2. Ibid., 4.
3. Ibid., 24.
4. James Carroll, "How Not to Tell a War Story," *Boston Globe*, May 3, 2010.
5. Walter Isaacson, *Steve Jobs* (New York: Simon & Schuster, 2011), 970.
6. Google Hans Rosling at www.ted.com.
7. Edward Tufte, *The Cognitive Style of PowerPoint*, 25 (Italics are the author's).
8. Ibid.

THIRTEEN
Everything Has Its Own Speed: Don't Kill the Butterfly

Life in the rush-rush, digitally driven world calls for educators to slow to the speed of things as they are.

Roberto rolls paint onto the ceiling of George Duncan's condo. Back and forth, back and forth, back and forth. Roberto is completing the final task that resulted from water damage. He lingers over each section until satisfied and then moves on. George is fascinated.

Roberto is a professional painter, a Brazilian who recently moved his family to George's city. He takes great pride in his work, something George senses the moment Roberto takes off his shoes and steps into the loft. He moves his lithe body quietly and efficiently as he lays tarps on the floor and places lightweight plastic on the furniture and cabinets. By early afternoon, he completes his prep work.

It is not until the next day that George pays closer attention to Roberto's technique. The painter caresses his painting pole with two hands and rhythmically rolls paint onto the ceiling. He takes his time over each portion and steps back to check his work. He paints sections of the wall in the same way. George wonders, "How is he able to accomplish so much while appearing to work at half the speed I would? Why does he do it in this way? Why doesn't he simply roll quickly and move on?"

As George observes Roberto's deliberate pace, he recalls an adage that he learned many years before in a philosophy class: "Everything has its own speed." Roberto embodies this truth. As he finishes, George wants to ask him about speed, but he's not sure that he can find the right words, as Roberto's native language is Portuguese. However, Roberto immediately understands George's question and its relationship to his work. "Yes," he says, "I know that about painting. You can't go faster than the paint."

Sometimes when George rinses dishes, he pays attention to how the water releases the food particles from each dish and thinks about everything having "its own speed." As he increases the water flow, the plate still rinses on its own. He notices the same effect when he washes his face and hands. Whenever he rushes, he splashes water, but when he lets the soap and water do what they do, his face and hands become clean with no spills.

Teaching is complicated but becomes more complicated when a teacher hurries. Sheila Webster, who teaches a fifth-grade self-contained class, felt ready to inspire her students on the first day that she began teaching three years ago. She was an eager learner in college. She pushed her teachers to stretch her thinking. Yet recently, she has noticed that whenever she presses her students, many of them begin to lose balance, develop anxieties, and become agitated.

One afternoon, toward the end of a particularly hectic day, Sheila asks her students to read quietly at their desks or on the floor. While observing them, she sees Jesse Palmer, a quiet and attentive student, not even halfway through a book that he began to read the week before. She ponders:

> "Why do I persist in trying to have my students complete tasks at the same time?" she asks herself. "Why don't I pay attention to the speed of each child?
>
> "Take Jesse sitting on the floor in the corner: so he reads slower than anyone in the class. What's wrong with that? Yet I keep trying to push him and all my students to work at the same pace. Look at him reading at his own pace! His introspective brain is obviously engaged.
>
> "He always seems to remember what he reads. Perhaps he is absorbing more than his quicker-reading classmates. Perhaps he is taking time to ponder related thoughts or connect his reading to previous knowledge. Or maybe he's asking himself questions."

As she comes out of her reverie, she realizes that students work at their own speed—and that she needs to pay attention to the speed of each one. When she pushes to complete a lesson, she often ends up far from her intentions. Students start to slip away. Some fall behind. Once they check out, she might as well stop. She now realizes that her push to complete her lessons interferes with the time everyone needs to arrive.

Now Sheila takes time to listen to her practice. Listening to herself and listening to her students keeps her in the moment. Because she now chooses to move at a pace that is in synch with her students, as difficult as it may be, she is confident that everyone will eventually arrive at their destination. She is grateful to Jesse Palmer, who showed her a better way to think about her teaching.

Not long after that, Sheila discovers Jennifer L. Robert's web talk "The Power of Patience."[1] Toward the beginning, Roberts shares an assignment that she gives to all her art history students: to do an intensive research study of one piece of art of their own choosing and then—here's where Sheila is most surprised—the student is to spend *three full hours* before the painting at its location, noting her observations while staying disconnected from her electronic devices. This process is about, in Robert's words, "deceleration, patience, and immersive attention."

Sheila knows that she could never do such an exercise with her students. She can, however, help them step away from the ubiquitous, instantaneous thrusts of a social-media–driven culture and take time to explore their thinking and imaginations.

She's already thinking about taking longer times when introducing students to new concepts. "Why not," she thinks to herself, "project an image of a pilgrim or of the moon and give my students five or ten minutes simply to look? No talking, just observing."

Teaching is an active verb. Every year it seems to Sheila and her colleagues that more curriculum is added to what they already teach. Outside pressures demand that they complete more in the same amount of time—and even in less time as more dates are added for federal and state assessments. They put pressure on themselves and feel guilty when they think they are falling behind—a guilt often fostered by the administration.

Often, when Sheila puts students to work in groups or individually, she travels around the room to nudge their learning. She likes interacting with them, asking questions, and offering suggestions. Now, she tends to be more gentle and stops to listen as well as to nudge. One day, because she needs to complete a task for the office, her student groups appear to function well without any prodding. "Perhaps," she says to herself, "I can step back even further and simply listen."

As she observes, she notices that some students prefer to work alone or in pairs, so she decides to make those options available. Sheila is learning to find balance—that middle place where she can bring learning to the students and, at the same time, bring students to the learning.

If Roberto's painting and Sheila's revelations do not invite principals and teachers to reconsider practice, perhaps Nikos Kazantzakis's words will:

> I remember one morning when I discovered a cocoon in the bark of a tree, just as a butterfly was making a hole in its case and preparing to come out. I waited a while, but it was too long appearing and I was impatient. I bent over it and breathed on it to warm it. I warmed it as quickly as I could and the miracle began to happen right before my eyes, faster than life. The case opened, the butterfly started slowly crawling out and I shall never forget my horror when I saw how its

> wings were folded back and crumpled; the wretched butterfly tried with its whole trembling body to unfold them. Bending over it, I tried to help with my breath. In vain.
>
> It needed to be hatched out patiently and the unfolding of the wings should be a gradual process in the sun. Now it was too late. My breath had forced the butterfly to appear, all crumpled, before its time. It struggled desperately and, a few seconds later, died in the palm of my hand.
>
> That little body is, I do believe, the greatest weight I have on my conscience. For I realize today that it is a mortal sin to violate the great laws of nature. We should not hurry, we should not be impatient, but we should obey the eternal rhythm.[2]

Kazantzakis implores us to "obey the eternal rhythm" and to care for and respect the needs of others. Sheila recalls hearing his message as a young teacher but did not pay much attention to it. At the time, she still had much to learn about listening, about everything at "its own speed." She had yet to absorb the concept of mindfulness that she discovered in Thich Nhat Hanh's wisdom about "washing the dishes to wash the dishes."[3]

Even now, she sometimes pushes rather than listens, coaxes rather than waits, prods rather than hesitates. She listens better but knows she could listen more.

Sheila understands the challenge of pacing her classroom. Often she feels pressure to cover material in a specified timeframe, particularly when unsuspected events drive her school day: A child loses composure; the fire alarm sounds; an angry parent bursts into her room; a lawnmower roars beneath her window; the principal calls over the intercom; and he calls again asking for her reports due yesterday.

Sheila wonders,

- "How can my colleagues and I find composure amidst these pressures?"
- "How can we become calm so our students can act at their own speed?"
- "How can we think "wash the dishes to wash the dishes" when our minds are flooded with the next thing to be done?"

In these moments, Sheila and her colleagues can choose to step back. Stepping back may provide a needed perspective and allow them to regain composure.

~ ~ ~

One evening, Sheila writes in her journal:

> In my early years of teaching, I frequently pushed beyond my children's speed and mine as well, which I now see created unnecessary

stress for all of us. My creativity needs to be in balance with my students' receptivity. I now take time to bring my ideas in harmony with their experience.

My best teaching depends upon how well I listen. And while I often come up short, I try to pay attention at every moment. As I reflect, it helps me from not acting in Kazantzakis's words, "faster than life." I do not want to kill the butterfly.

POINTS TO PURSUE

The universe at "its own speed"

Thinking about Roberto, the painter who does not go "faster than the paint," have you ever thought of the universe having "its own speed"? That everything not only has a beginning and end but also has its own defined time limits? From cells, to planets, to the sun? Have you had a revelation similar to Sheila Webster's in this chapter? If you believe that each student acts at his own speed, how does it affect your teaching?

Deceleration, patience, immersive attention

What was your first reaction to Jennifer Roberts's assignment to her students to sit in front of a painting for *three hours*? Does this assignment give you ideas to try with your students? Can you imagine providing your students with longer times to concentrate? Do you have the patience to teach them how? Would it be worth it in today's fast, digitally driven culture?

Prod less

How can you allow time for students to be as they are, as Sheila unintentionally does one afternoon? Simply to take time to witness, particularly when you feel pressure to prod and coax?

When is it best to let students be? How can you discipline yourself to do just that? As a colleague said to me, how you can be the "guide on the side" rather than "teacher as preacher?"[4]

Unfold rather than infuse

Given the constant temptation to tell students what to learn and when, can you take Nikos Kazantzakis's words to heart and let the cocoon of each student unfold naturally? Can you find the patience, through more listening perhaps, to watch, rather than trying to force learning? Can you do this in a pressure-filled environment?

"Wash the dishes to wash the dishes"

Can Thich Nhat Hanh's admonition to "wash the dishes to wash the dishes" help you become more patient, not only with your students but with yourself? Take time after a meal to "wash the dishes to wash the dishes" and not think about what you will do afterward. Simply pay attention. Invite your students to do the same with their homework.

Seek composure

What interferes the most in your life as a teacher or principal? A distraught child? An angry parent? A sudden call to the superintendent's office? How can you ameliorate your anxieties? How can you find balance, a sense that "everything has its own speed," and discover the composure you need to do your job well?

Establish a dialogue with other teachers with your ideas. Log on to Teachingthatmatters.wordpress.com and join the conversation.

NOTES

1. Jennifer L. Roberts at the Harvard Initiative for Learning and Teaching (HILT) conference, May 2013, http://harvardmagazine.com/2013/11/the-power-of-patience.
2. Nikos Kazantzakis, *Zorba the Greek*. I received this excerpt from a friend early in my teaching. It can now be found on the web.
3. Thich Nhat Hanh, *The Miracle of Mindfulness*, 3–4.
4. Frank Gould, in a personal correspondance.

FOURTEEN

The Four Agreements: Find Your Center

Wisdom from the ancients and mystics invites us to find solace and center ourselves in our work. These Four Agreements provide one such path.

We live in interesting times. Corporate messages bombard us on television, radio, the Internet, magazines, billboards, cell phones—virtually everywhere. We feel the chaos. We wonder where we can find respite.

Teachers work in chaotic environments. Chaos can overwhelm, some days more than others. Many choose to seek wisdom in order to find peace in their practice. Some seek it from a partner, friends, or colleagues. Others choose different paths, such as sitting alone after school in their classroom, taking a walk by the ocean or on a mountain path, sitting in a meditation community, musing in a park, reading poetry, or watching films—and sometimes from teaching itself.

And, once in a while, insights appear over the transom. Don Miguel Ruiz's *The Four Agreements* becomes one such gift for Walter Brooks, as it practically falls off a shelf into his hands in his favorite bookstore. A middle school social studies teacher at a private school, he often peruses spiritual book sections, because he wants to find wisdom to help him be more patient with his eighth graders—and himself.

For nearly thirty years, Walter has been looking for meaning behind the obvious. He has experimented with different approaches to teaching including, "Man: A Course of Study,"[1] "Earthship,"[2] "Going West,"[3] and "Facing History and Ourselves"[4]—and he creates innovative units of his own. He discovers his love for ancient philosophers when he introduces his students to Confucius, Lao Tzu, and the Buddha. He finds that he learns as much as they do—perhaps even more.

The Four Agreements is a small book, fewer than one hundred and forty pages in a five-by-seven-inch, large-print format, in which Don Miguel Ruiz, a Mexican Toltec master, offers "a personal guide to freedom." "A tall order from such a small venue," thinks Walter.[5]

The Four Agreements themselves are straightforward. Yet, Walter realizes that he needs several readings to absorb their true meaning. They are:

1. Be impeccable with your word.
2. Don't take anything personally.
3. Don't make assumptions.
4. Always do your best.

BE IMPECCABLE WITH YOUR WORD

The first Agreement means to speak with integrity, to say what we mean. Walter's parents often taught him the back side of this Agreement, not to tell lies. He remembers falling short, however, whenever he thought that he'd be better off not telling the truth—or the whole truth. White lies often seemed to work.

Ruiz moves beyond this simpler meaning and states that to *be impeccable with your word* means that we do not gossip about others *or* speak against ourselves. We begin with our own impeccable thinking, thought words, and internal conversations. From these come our spoken words. We choose to use the power of our words in the direction of truth and love. Walter knows that the words he speaks become seeds for his students and for himself.

Walter agrees that the same holds true for listening. When he hears others speak about him, he knows that he needs to be impeccable as he listens. He does not believe what is not true, because internalizing untruths, especially about him, is harmful. The giver of gossip does not succeed unless the receiver accepts it. "Being vigilant about truth," Walter thinks, "whether I am speaking or listening, demands that I be impeccable with my word."

"When you are impeccable," Ruiz writes, "you take responsibility for your actions, but you do not judge or blame yourself."[6] Walter takes responsibility for his actions, but, he struggles with self-judgment. He tends to hear censure worse than it is, and he looks for praise when he feels he's "done good," as his father used to say. Given that teachers are frequently blamed for society's failures, it's no wonder that Walter and many of his colleagues are sensitive to criticism and seek active public support.

Sometimes, Walter thinks it might be better to say less. But then he wonders if he is he being impeccable with his word? "Is it possible,"

Walter wonders, "to be impeccable when I choose not to say what I think?" Perhaps he's being impeccable with his thoughts.

DON'T TAKE ANYTHING PERSONALLY

When Walter was young, he believed what others said about him, especially his parents. He was an active boy, often getting into mischief, so he probably collected more criticism from his parents than his friends. He saw that his friends were also living with admonitions from parents, teachers, and other adults. Life seemed to work that way. No doubt, Walter thinks, he now has a similar influence on his students.[7]

In this second Agreement *don't take anything personally*, Ruiz offers a way out from under the influence of others—a way in which to become true to ourselves. When we take things personally, Ruiz argues, we agree with what people say about us. It becomes a matter of "personal importance," where everything is "about me." We think that we are responsible for everything. Ultimately, Ruiz says—and here he surprises—taking everything personally is a matter of maximum selfishness.[8]

Walter feels vulnerable as he strains to keep this Agreement. He hears painful comments about him and his colleagues from students, parents, supervisors—and even in the news. And sometimes, he feels caught in conundrums and chooses to take blame for something, even when untrue. When he takes blame, he realizes that he is taking it personally.

Yet Walter knows that when he hears a comment directed to him, the person is also talking about himself. The same is true when he says something to another.

Ruiz points out that when we agree with opinions that hurt us, we allow them to become poison. He urges us not to aim to earn other people's acceptance. Our goal is to live in our own movie—accept ourselves, and live with love and without fear.

"When we are immune to the opinions and actions of others, we won't be the victim of needless suffering."[9] Walter intends to explore the idea of living in his own movie as a way to not take things personally.

Ultimately, not taking anything personally, Walter concludes, gives him a personal freedom. Gaining personal freedom, after all, *is* the underlying message of *The Four Agreements*. This Agreement invites him and his colleagues to trust themselves to make responsible choices. He believes in accepting his choices and not letting others decide for him.

DON'T MAKE ASSUMPTIONS

> One thing, Mr. Brooks, that bothered me when I was in your eighth-grade social studies class was that you seemed to decide early on which of us was smarter and which were not—and you never changed your mind!

Hilary's insight, coming from someone who was an eighth grader nearly thirty years ago, was an epiphany for Walter. From that moment, he decided he would try to remain open to each of his students' potential every day and not make assumptions about them. He wanted to see them as they were and not as he thought they should be.

"We have a tendency to make assumptions about everything," Ruiz writes. "The problem with making assumptions is that we *believe* that they are the truth."[10] Ruiz helped Walter understand that he should hesitate before reacting whenever he thinks someone is making assumptions about him.

Before becoming upset, Walter chooses to be gentle with perceived offenders and ask clarifying questions. As he does, he knows he will have a piece of the personal freedom that Ruiz wants for him and everyone.

In terms of relationships, Ruiz writes, "Real love is accepting other people the way they are without trying to change them. If we try to change them, it means we don't really like them."[11] Strong words. Walter wonders as a teacher,

- "If I try to change my students, does that really mean that I'm not loving them?
- What is the line between my insistence on what I want from my students and what I am asking from them?
- How can my teaching be an act of love, if my aim is in part to change some students?
- If my instruction invites, encourages, and accepts what is at the moment, could it then be considered loving?"

Ruiz offers clear advice for Walter:

> Find the courage to ask questions and express what you really want. Communicate with others as clearly as you can to avoid misunderstandings, sadness, and drama. With just this one Agreement, you can completely transform your life.[12]

Walter decides to place these words in front of his teaching binder alongside Elspeth Campbell Murphy's "If I were a student in my classroom, would I want to return tomorrow?" Together these statements serve as a daily reminder to maintain his integrity with all of his students.

ALWAYS DO YOUR BEST

To do our best is a fluid process. Ruiz makes clear that any efforts to fulfill this fourth Agreement can be good at times and not so good at other times. But, the important point he makes is that we must commit to it every minute. If we do our best, we will not be judging ourselves. We should not decide to do our best because we want to earn an award or recognition. As the Bhagavad Gita states, we should not become attached to our results.

Ruiz invites us to live inside a three-part paradigm:

1. when we like what we do, we do our best and enjoy life;
2. when we enjoy our life, we do our best;
3. we can only be ourselves when we do our best.[13]

"What would happen," Walter wonders, "if I invite my students to live in this paradigm? I know that I teach in a school culture in which my colleagues and I feel we often have to do the bidding of those in charge. In this context, can I make my classroom a space where everyone likes what they do—are free to be themselves—and get done what needs to be done?"

Ruiz's statement, "Action makes the difference,"[14] means that doing your best in whatever endeavor leads to mastery—and supports your efforts to live the other three Agreements. Of all the Agreements, the fourth may be the most straightforward and obvious. Yet, Ruiz cautions us to be vigilant, because we can easily fail when we decide to take shortcuts, cut corners, make wrong turns, and act slothful.

Walter recalls that, as a young teacher aiming to earn a professional contract, he was driven to do his best to impress students, colleagues, and supervisors. Secure with tenure, he continues to make a conscious effort to do his best, even though no one pays much attention to his teaching. In his last years, he intends to be conscientious, unlike some teachers he's seen close to retirement. They tend to tread water.

Toward the end of his book Ruiz invites readers to make another Agreement, "I choose to honor the Four Agreements."[15] To make this deeper commitment, he cautions that to do our best, we know that sometimes we succeed and other times we don't. Knowing that we are doing our best allows us to pursue this path without self-judgment.

Ruiz concludes that each of us is ultimately responsible for our own freedom. As a Toltec, Ruiz lives with no leaders and no followers, "where you have your own truth and live your truth."[16] To find personal freedom is a choice.

When we agree to live with the Four Agreements, we learn to love ourselves. To love ourselves allows us to love others—and loving others helps us love ourselves. How we live with ourselves is how we treat others.

Walter commits to live the Four Agreements in his classroom. He knows that sharing his choice to seek personal freedom through his actions lets his students know that they can seek theirs. He is impeccable with his word, does not react personally, avoids making assumptions, and always does his best. When a child lies, he speaks truth. When a child swears, he holds his tongue. When a child hates, he loves. And when a child fails to try, he encourages.

Ruiz invites readers to create their own path to internalize his Four Agreements. His guidance offers teachers solace as they cope with the endless complexities of school life. His words allow teachers to remember who they are, what they value, and what they want. Walter is grateful for the gift of *The Four Agreements*.

POINTS TO PURSUE

"We live in interesting times."

The paraphrasing of Confucius's aphorism, "May you live in interesting times," opens this chapter. It sets the tone of the fast-driven, complex culture in which we live. Do you feel beaten by its chaotic energy? Do you feel overwhelmed at times? Have you sought solace from the endless proliferation of events that seem to fold in on themselves?

Walter Brooks believes he was given *The Four Agreements* as a gift. Have you found a similar gift for your life? If you've not found solace for yourself, do you know what you are looking for?

Seek to be impeccable with your word

To be impeccable with your word takes courage. How do you know when you are impeccable with yourself? With your students? Can you be as attentive to what you hear others say to one another as you are to what you hear what others say to you? Who can help you determine if you are impeccable with your word?

Live in your own movie

When you truly understand that you live in your own movie and let others live in theirs, you do not take anything personally. When you hear someone say something about you, can you remember that it's their movie? When you do, you will become freer to remember who you are and not what others choose to say or believe about you.

Have you thought of the scenario of being-in-your-own-movie? If you haven't, and particularly if you tend to take things personally, give it a try and see how this paradigm works for you and others around you.

Avoid making assumptions

Making assumptions is a more common practice than people realize. As a principal or teacher, you will better serve your school if you choose not to make assumptions when you think or speak about another, particularly about your students.

If you feel that others tend to make assumptions about you or your students, inquire to find out whether it is true or not before you make assumptions about what they are saying.

Discover when you are doing your best

How do you know when you do your best? Simply to believe that you are may not be enough. How can you better assess yourself? Who can help you?

Personal beliefs and the classroom

In this chapter, Walter Brooks gets it right. He understands that he cannot proselytize to his students his commitment to the Four Agreements, but he does realize that he can live them. He can, as stated at the end of the chapter, be impeccable with his word, not react personally, avoid making assumptions, and always do his best.

He knows that "when a child lies, he speaks truth. When a child swears, he holds his tongue. When a child hates, he loves. And when a child fails to try, he encourages."

He feels that following these Agreements has made him a better teacher. Have you found a path that helps you be a better teacher in your classroom, in your school?

Assess the Four Agreements for yourself

Which Agreement is easiest for you? Which is the most difficult? Have a conversation with a colleague about your answers and ask them for theirs. Does this help you better understand The Four Agreements and your relationship with them?[17]

Establish a dialogue with other teachers with your ideas. Log on to Teachingthatmatters.wordpress.com and join the conversation.

NOTES

1. "Man: A Course of Study" (MACOS), Educational Services Incorporated, ESI, (now Educational Development Center, EDC), Cambridge, MA, 1964.
2. James Oswald, *Earthship: Four Dimensional Fluid Geography of Spaceship Earth* (New York: Institute for World Order, 1974).
3. James Abbot, "Going West" (Hanover, NH, 1977). An extensive simulation game that Jim Abbot developed for midddle school.
4. "Facing History and Ourselves" (Brookline, MA), https://www.facinghistory.org.
5. Don Miguel Ruiz, *The Four Agreements: A Toltec Wisdom Book* (San Rafael, CA: Allen-Amber, 1997).
6. Ibid., 31.
7. Ibid., 1–23, Ruiz's first chapter "Domestication and the Dream of the Planet."
8. Ibid., 48.
9. Ibid., inside front cover.
10. Ibid., 63.
11. Ibid., 70.
12. Ibid., from the book jacket
13. Ibid., 80–1.
14. Ibid., 86.
15. Ibid., 88.
16. Ibid., 100.
17. This idea came from Carl Marsack in a personal conversation.

IV

Write Letters

> I like a teacher who gives you something to take home to think about besides homework. —Lily Tomlin

Thoughtful letters provide teachers encouragement and guide them to become open to what is and discover new directions.

Part IV has three such letters.

When a letter arrives in the mail, unlike with e-mail, we pause and take time to open it. Often we sit down before beginning to read, anticipating something important. Letters have been like that for generations. When we sit down to write a letter, we have a similar experience. We see ourselves slowing down, taking cognizance of each word we write. Our mind slows, reflects, and releases our thoughts, word by word.

Fritz Thomas, a lifelong middle school teacher and now a teacher of teachers, writes letters. As a teacher, he often wrote to his students at the end of the year. He wanted to let them know, beyond their grades, his impressions of their presence in his classroom. While it took time, he found the writing deeply satisfying.

Now, as a consultant, after professional development workshops and courses, he often writes letters to participants as e-mail attachments. He feels that writing allows him to discover hidden gems in the landscape of his mind.

He writes because he wants participants to try out the ideas and strategies that he and they generated and at the same time show his respect for the work that they do. He finds that writing forces him to reflect as much as narrate. As he writes, insights emerge from the depths of his imagination. He feels that he gains as much from writing these letters as he hopes participants will gain from reading them.

Teaching That Matters: Engaging Minds, Improving Schools is a lengthy reflection—a long letter if you will—that pulls together insights from the abundant wisdom of teachers. The letters to Alicia, Peter, and Pamela are composites of letters that Fritz has written. They illustrate the potential of words that can lead them—and him—to personal reflection and change.

FIFTEEN
Letter to Alicia: Celebrate Your Uniqueness

A consultant's letter of encouragement to Alicia, a new teacher, in support of her desire to keep her uniqueness inside an embedded traditional school culture.

Dear Alicia,

I appreciate your thoughtful e-mail. Not often do teachers take time to write, especially to a consultant. Given that I will not be at your school until next week, I've decided to respond to your concerns immediately.

You indicate that you often feel like you are being tossed about by challenges and surprises. I hope this letter encourages you to discover the larger picture of your first year. I hope, as well, that you will feel free to discuss these ideas with your fellow new teachers. When you choose to reflect together, you are better able to collect your thoughts. You come to see the trees in the forest.

What do you remember, Alicia, about one of your favorite teachers? Perhaps you recall her presence, her being there for you and your classmates. She told stories around what she taught. Her persona was hers alone, her style unique. You felt welcomed every day and left each class with something to remember. You worked hard for her, and she worked hard for you. She seemed to know you better than you knew yourself. She cared about everyone.

Despite public perceptions to the contrary, teaching is a deeply personal pursuit. In your choice to come to your school, you are not simply replacing another teacher. You bring your special self. You say and do what no one else has ever done. Even if you teach the same subject with the same texts and materials as she did, you teach who *you* are every day.[1]

You remember how often you were assigned a seat when you attended in school. It must seem almost like yesterday. Once you sit at your desk you look up to see the teacher standing at the front asking you to quiet down. You notice questions, quotations, or scribbles from previous classes across the blackboard. An American flag stands in a front corner, an intercom near the door, the shades partially drawn, and fluorescent ceiling lights on.

The teacher takes attendance, makes announcements, collects and passes back homework, answers any homework questions, and gives the lesson of the day. Just before the end of class, she tells you to copy down the assignment from the board, and if there is time, she allows you to begin. When the bell rings, you stand up to leave.

Still, no doubt you remember teachers who you felt were special. Although you and your classmates may have preferred different teachers, you usually agreed on their good qualities. You knew that they

- connected with you personally—or made every effort to;
- taught you something to remember—at least you could feel their urging;
- engaged you—hardly a lesson passed without the teacher posing an intriguing question or a perplexing problem;
- surprised you—never seemed to settle into a rut;
- had a sense of humor—and fit it into their teaching; and
- knew you by name—and knew you well.

Alicia, you've told me that you want to create a classroom that is special, as "one less traveled by." Yet you've said that your students act restless and standoffish. They seem not to care about school. Some slouch in their seats, put their heads on their desks, shout out, annoy fellow students, leave their seats without permission, and attempt to text. You notice that some of them make no effort to participate in class or pass in homework.

Sometimes it seems as if you are not in the room. Perhaps they wonder whether you are for real, so they may be testing you. Despite their negative demeanor, they may be looking for ways to connect with you.

You've indicated that you are afraid to let the administration know just how difficult these students are. You've heard that if you send them to the office too often, the administration may think of you as a poor teacher. Yet, if you do not find some way to constrain these students, you will be unable to teach. You signed a contract, after all, to be a teacher, and a good one at that. Asking for help was not part of the contract. You feel stuck.

You realize, too, that you are in a school culture that expects teachers to take care of their own problems. Still, you are not sure how to act. I suggest that you share your concerns with your fellow new teachers.

Joe Reynolds, who teaches with you in the sixth grade, could be a good person in whom to confide. In our workshops, he often supports your point of view. He may well be having the same issues with his students. You can ask for help from each other. If together you decide to approach your administrators, they may be less likely to assume that you are not doing your jobs well.

Some school cultures are difficult to break into, particularly ones like yours that give new teachers multiple class preps and difficult students. You have three preps—too many—and some difficult students but apparently not any more than your fellow new teachers.

You have said that you want to create a safe classroom so you can enliven your lessons. You might begin by breaking up your routine. At the start of a class, for example, instead of going over the homework, you might open with a rigorous question to encourage serious debate.

You could ask Margaret Rivers, who teaches social studies, to share her four-corners exercise with you. I've seen her do it and it works well. (See page xii for a description of Margaret's lesson.) Or, you could decide to dress up as a character in the book that you are teaching. You could rearrange your desks. Or, as students walk in the door, you might flash a video clip to energize their thinking about yesterday's lesson.

As we discussed at our workshops before school, you and your fellow new teachers are entering a new era. Remember what I shared in your packet? We had quite a discussion.

> We are at the vortex of a radical shift in our culture. Unless we respond with intelligence, creativity, and commitment, our students will zoom past us, ignoring our outmoded methods and approaches. They will find ways to educate themselves, as have all pioneers who invent solutions to newfound problems.
>
> We will need to collaborate to create ways for meeting today's students where they are and nurture them to become good students, good citizens, and good people. This is not about indulgence. We have much to offer—and we need to decide just what that is.

You remember, too, before the beginning of school that you and your new-teacher colleagues spoke in superlatives about your prospects in the classroom. You spoke as if being a teacher would somehow invoke magic in your students from the first day. The reality, as you have already discovered and as the research confirms, is that within the first month— and in the first days sometimes—you slip from your "fantasies" into what Harry Wong calls "survival." The struggle of real teaching begins.

Wong's research, however, lets you know that short-term struggles can lead to long-term success. With patience, support, and some luck along the way, he notes that you can reach "mastery" and later have "impact" beyond your wildest expectations.[2]

You write in your email that, by the time you step into your car at the end of the day, you are often more tired than you imagined possible. You ask yourself, "How can I keep this up? What can I do to win these kids over? What do I do wrong? Who can I turn to?"

Remember, as I suggested, don't forget first to celebrate what went well for you and your students. Such as the day you told me about your principal telling you that she likes your upbeat attitude. Or when you were excited that Johnny came back after skipping school for two weeks. And how pleased you were that Rita earned her first A after only earning C's. Make celebration a part of your every day. It will sustain you through hard times.

When you feel really down, step back and visualize one of your students sitting at his desk. Remind yourself that he sits there every day for forty-five minutes in most of his classes (not always in yours). Remember, too, in these classrooms he looks at the backs of the heads of his classmates.

As you discover your empathy, you will feel more respect for him. You'll realize that you are doing everything possible to break the monotony of school for him and his classmates—and for yourself—and you have no intentiom to give up. You'll feel better.

Alicia, you know full well that if you talk at your students you cannot compete with their darting minds. You know that you have to bring new ideas and approaches to the table. You'll have to be far more inventive than your teachers ever were if you are to gain your students' respect and confidence.

Pay attention, then, as you step away from the podium, from that symbol of delivery, and commit to engage every student. You know that if you don't, you will lose any chance of being their teacher. You didn't become a teacher to have that happen.

I've written more than I intended. I hope, however, that it helps.
Sincerely,
Fritz

POINTS TO PURSUE

Teachers—and then there are teachers

The letter to Alicia opens by addressing the teaching profession. It asks her to recall her favorite teachers, something that all of us can do. It reminds her that teaching is deeply personal. Yet the letter also takes into account the many teachers who replicate embedded traditional teaching patterns every day. It then comes full circle, listing the qualities of special teachers.

Have you taken an inventory of yourself as a teacher? Have you stepped back to see the patterns of your classroom and how you perpetuate them? Have you thought about what makes a teacher special? About what makes you special? (Check the list given in the letter.)

Seek to understand how today's students are different

Throughout the book, it makes references to characteristics of today's students. Alicia sees them "slouch in their seats, put their heads on their desks, ... attempt to text."

What differences do you see in your students? Besides their apparent inability to pay attention (a common complaint among seasoned teachers), how else are they different from how you saw yourself at their age? What are their strengths? What do they pay attention to?

How can you capitalize on who they are, on what they bring, rather than complain that they are unreachable?

Seek discipline help

If you believe that your principal will judge you if you tell him that you are having trouble with discipline, how will you get help? How will you accept that teaching alone does not mean that you should be expected to do everything well, especially when you are new?

How can you convince your colleagues that your students and their students belong to all of you? How might this mindset improve classroom behavior?

New teachers' early struggles

Alicia, like so many new teachers, has too many preps. From her first day, she feels overwhelmed with all she has to do. She finds that her early enthusiasm quickly wanes as she struggles to engage her students.

What have you done as a new teacher to connect with your students? Have you sought help from veterans? Are you willing to take risks and, if necessary, step out from the culture of teaching in your school?

As a veteran, what have you done to help your new teachers succeed? They are, after all, the future lifeblood of your school.

Celebrate your teaching

How can you as a new teacher see yourself as special, not as "just a teacher"? How do you remind yourself every day that you are unique, that you are who you are, that you make a difference? Do you celebrate your accomplishments at the end of every day?

Empathize with students

Students struggle to make school suit them. After all, they have ways to learn by themselves. They can reach the world on their cell phones! How can you help them want to spend quality time with you in the classroom? Simple question, difficult solutions.

Claim and sustain your uniqueness

The concluding paragraph of the letter reminds Alicia that "You'll have to be far more inventive than your teachers ever were if you are to gain your students' respect and confidence."

Teachers often state that the divide between them and their students is widening. Do you agree? What do you do to intrigue student to want to learn your lessons? How can you win their confidence?

Establish a dialogue with other teachers with your ideas. Log on to Teachingthatmatters.wordpress.com and join the conversation.

NOTES

1. See Parker Palmer, *The Courage to Teach* (Jossey Bass, 10th Anniversary Edition, 2007) for a comprehensive understanding of the idea that we teach who we are.

2. Harry K. Wong and Rosemary T. Wong, *How To Be an Effective Teacher: The First Days of School* (Mountain View, CA: Harry K. Wong, 1998), 5–6. Wong's four stages of teaching: fantasy, survival, mastery, and impact. This book is probably the best known beginning-teachers manual. Many readers seem to agree, as more than 3.5 million copies have been sold.

SIXTEEN
Letter to Peter: Be Yourself

A consultant's advice to a young teacher, Peter, helps him understand that positive change in schools can happen one teacher at a time.

Dear Peter,

Thank you for letting me know about the new ideas that you have created. They sound intriguing! However, I am sorry that you are frustrated with your continued perception of the quality of teaching in your school. You think that many of your colleagues pay more attention to what *they* are doing rather than to what their *students* are learning. Teaching for them appears to be more like *delivery* than *engagement*.

Why do you think most of your colleagues persist in teaching the same way? What keeps them locked into this paradigm? What will release them from the tyranny of the obsolete, ineffective, tiresome, stale, repetitive, outmoded, boring, monotonous, tedious, uninspired, irksome, dreary, vapid, vacuous, banal, dull, dreary, and plain-vanilla patter of spewed strings of sentences one class period after another—day after day, year after year?

Pardon my rant, Peter, but I have seen this dance since I sat at my desk in first grade. Your colleague, Marco Enzo, reminds me of many high school colleagues who insisted upon lecturing.

In a recent conversation, Marco argued that lectures, despite increasing evidence to the contrary, prepare his students for college, He said that his students do not work well in small groups, as they lose focus and become disruptive. I've tried to convince him that he could structure different types of lessons, but he said he'd already tried them. Frankly, I think he lectures every day because it's easier for him than designing interactive lessons.

I don't mean to sound cynical, as I know of many teachers who do their best to encourage student involvement; you have some in your school. When they give lectures, they make them engaging with illustrations and anecdotes—and some of them even provide intervals during class for processing. They also invoke a variety of learning formats including small groups, triads, pairs, and opportunities for personal reflection. They recognize that students have a wide range of learning preferences.

I sense that they are aware that one-third to one-half of their students may be introverts, and therefore they need to respond to their needs as well to the more sociable students.[1] I know that you have.

Yet I imagine that you have been tempted to pull back and be more traditional. You might then be seen more as a team player and no longer be given dirty looks at faculty meetings. Like that time last year when you dared to speak up about extending the school day so that you could have longer class periods. That must have been hard.

You've observed that most of the young teachers in your school have stuck with whole-class, lecture-style lessons. You've mentioned your good friend Bill Noyes who's told you that he's more comfortable when he faces his students to keep their attention. He says that he's tried to use small groups but quickly gives up when his students become unruly. He does not want administrators to see his classes out of control and conclude that he is a poor teacher.

Besides, he believes that teaching in the traditional manner is the way that most students know—and that he will have a better chance of fitting into the school's culture and have his contract renewed. While you disagree with his reasons, you understand them.

You listen to Bill complain about student apathy. Like you, he sees boys in their oversized shirts and jackets slink down at their desks while girls endlessly twirl their hair and roll their eyes. He watches them pass notes and attempt to text from their pockets. He observes seas of blank faces. No engagement. Nobody home.

No matter how fast he talks, no matter how intense he tries to deliver material, he says that he feels lucky to reach a few of his students. By the end of class, no doubt he begins to feel some relief. At the bell, he takes a deep breath in anticipation of the next group. He turns back to the first page of his notes ready to begin again.

The way I see it, Bill and teachers like him deliver hamster-wheel-driven lessons that spin endlessly with no time for comprehension and understanding. No wonder students check out. I wonder, too, how soon Bill will burn out.

In the faculty room, you hear veteran teachers express frustration about the public's complaints about poor teaching. You notice, however, that the biggest complainers are those few teachers who arrive just before school begins and follow their students out of the building at the closing bell. They treat teaching as time-clock job.

They are the first to complain when asked to try new approaches, new curricula, or to work in new team or grade. Their response is often, "Oh, we've tried that, but it didn't work." They prefer to do tomorrow what they did today and yesterday—an endless loop of mediocrity.

In virtually every school in which I consult, I hear how highly the faculty and staff perceive themselves. They see their camaraderie as evidence of how competent they are and how lucky their students and parents are. They develop strong *congeniality*—long a trademark of the profession.

However, as far as I can see, most faculties rarely move beyond social bonding to make the commitment to develop serious *collegiality* that aims to improve instruction. And teaching in their isolated classrooms, unfortunately, assures that they can teach without anyone else knowing what they actually are doing.

Teaching, as you well know, is not about feeling comfortable. It's about what happens to students. It takes courage to be yourself, especially as a second-year teacher. You've accepted that not all of your colleagues appreciate you.

And, you have made an important choice. You intend to pursue your own ideas and not retreat and do school as it was done to you. You want to find the real teacher within you. I know that you will persist and, in the process, discover ways to meet your students halfway—more than halfway when necessary.

As I have said to you and your fellow newer teachers, classroom change happens one classroom at a time. No number of mandates will force teachers to teach differently. Only when principals and teachers decide to make changes do changes actually take place. Hence, I encourage you to continue to pursue your chosen path.

Sincerely,
Fritz

POINTS TO PURSUE

The persistence of old ways

Peter's good friend, Bill Noyes, persists in teaching as he was taught. Despite his frustrations with poor responses from his students, he continues to deliver one lecture after another. He gives Peter a clear rationale for persisting in this manner. Peter thinks that Bill may think it's easier to teach this way.

Do you think it's fair to say that Bill (and colleagues like him) "deliver hamster-wheel-driven lessons that spin endlessly with no time for comprehension and understanding"? Are they really trapped inside a world of their own making that appears not to include the students they are serving?

Be willing to see students as they are

Bill Noyes is not alone in seeing his students acting apathetic, but he appears unwilling to change his practice in hopes of engaging them. He could begin by asking his students what bothers them, what they find distasteful in his class, what concerns they have about school. He could then ask them for ideas to make his lessons better and adopt those that he thinks might work.

Have you taken time to have metacognitive conservations with your students about improving your teaching?

Culture of the faculty room

The faculty room manifests the school's culture. Here teachers speak their minds on any and all issues. Teachers vent their concerns about the administration, students, the school board, and community. The underlying assumption behind these conversations is that what's said there stays there. Some teachers avoid going into those faculty rooms where complainers dominate.

What is the role of the complaining culture in your school? Do these teachers put a kibosh on new ideas? Do they lead resistance to change? What can you do to free them from this restrictive paradigm and become more open to consider better ways of teaching?

Shift from congeniality to collegiality

Faculties often see themselves as excellent. Yet, they remain in isolated classrooms and rarely see each other's teaching. What do you think could be done in your school to move your faculty from *congeniality* toward true *collegiality*—to become open to honest feedback from each other about what matters in teaching? What might you do to facilitate this process?

Be a force of one if need be

Peter is one teacher. Judging from his comments—and from that day in a faculty meeting—he appears somewhat alone. Undoubtedly, he's been tempted to pull back from his more radical practice and become more of a team player. He might well feel better being a part of the group. Yet he may, hopefully, decide to stay on his chosen path.

If you relate to Peter's dilemma, what could you do as a force of one, to paraphrase Gandhi, to become the change you wish to see in your school? How might you influence others to join you?

Establish a dialogue with other teachers with your ideas. Log on to Teachingthatmatters.wordpress.com and join the conversation.

NOTE

1. Susan Cain, *Quiet*, 255.

SEVENTEEN

Letter to Pamela: Make Relationships Your Priority

A consultant's letter to a former new teacher, Pamela, illustrates that strong student relationships are the basis for good classroom management.

Dear Pamela,

I have a confession to make. It's been more than a dozen years since I taught my first beginning-teachers class with you and your colleagues. I now believe I may have misled you, unintentionally perhaps, but misled nonetheless. In preparation for our before-school meetings, my company provided me with packets to give you that included ideas for good teaching based on research.

I especially recall sharing Harry Wong's formulas (as I judged them to be at the time), formulas designed to develop a well-managed classroom—what he called "a well-oiled machine." Although I thought that Wong's approach was simplistic, I shared it with you nonetheless.

Take Wong's idea that teachers must establish rules, procedures, and routines during the first days of school. He argues that teachers establish them before they attempt to teach lessons. I agree. It's certainly logical—and obvious—that a well-managed classroom is essential if students are to have any chance to learn. Yet, as I remember, Wong also did not choose to emphasize the importance of immediately establishing good relationships with students.

In my early years as a teacher, I never considered the need to set up Wong's parameters for the first days of school. I stepped into my first classroom, now more than fifty years ago, and fully expected students to arrive ready to learn—or at least to give me a chance to encourage them to. I hardly paid attention to rules and procedures. Perhaps, it was because I taught in an environment in which students and parents respected teachers.

When students misbehaved, my colleagues and I simply dealt with them. Sometimes we kept them after school, physically intervened in disputes, occasionally sent them to the office, or called their parents who would always back us up.

In that first year, I based my lessons on how my teachers had taught me. I assigned seats; took attendance; collected homework; called only on raised hands; passed out paper; administered bathroom and library passes; put information and assignments on the board; passed back tests and papers, etc. I knew the routine and so did my students.

In my second year when I moved from ninth grade to eighth, my department head asked me to invent an "area studies" course that would intrigue students, so I dispensed with many of those routines. Later, I taught in a progressive primary school in Leicestershire, England, and returned to the United States to teach in a fifth–sixth, progressive elementary school. In both of these instances, my colleagues and I needed to reinvent school as we knew it. If we had known more of Harry Wong's ideas, we might have been more articulate as to how to develop new procedures and routines.

But, as I reflect on my workshops with you and your colleagues, Pamela, I wonder if the packets' emphasis on classroom management was the right message. I wonder if I balanced that with my own deeply held principle of connecting with students: knowing their names, their interests, their willingness to learn, etc.

I wonder, too, if our focus on gaining extrinsic control of the classroom may have seemed more important than building relationships with each student. I might even have unwittingly instilled the notion that only students who exhibit good behavior earn rewards and those who do not suffer consequences (not punishment, of course, as we discussed at length).

The more I think about it, I wonder if the emphasis on the packets that we used might have unintentionally led you to develop a teacher-versus-student relationship in which the teacher acts as a *judge* rather than as a *mentor* who teaches students to learn how to gain control of their behaviors.

Unless you establish this priority, an early insistence on rules, procedures, and routines may send a wrong signal to your students. When done rigidly, which can happen if a teacher lacks confidence, students might well become alienated; her pressure to control increases tensions and the situation worsens. But when she strives to make good relationships a priority, she will more likely build a successful classroom. I sense that you know that.

The best approach, as you may well know by now, incorporates both of these priorities. The teacher specifies sensible parameters for a well-managed classroom—preferably in conversation with her students—and at the same time expresses delight at being their teacher. She greets them by name at the door, asks about their lives, listens to their stories, and tells her own.

When students disrupt, she waits patiently and respectfully admonishes when necessary. She never loses her temper, as she knows she may lose the respect of the class. To establish this balance is certainly a challenge but essential for a successful classroom.

She extends her relationship-building efforts beyond the classroom into the halls, into the cafeteria, onto the playing fields, to concerts and plays, and onto the street and into shops. If possible, she makes connections with future students and says how much she looks forward to being with them. She might even say, "I'm eager to get to know your mind."

Students pay attention to teachers' reputations. No doubt, Pamela, you now meet new students who already know about you—and you about them. You understand that a teacher can use her reputation to set a positive tone. She can let students know from the first day that their place in the classroom depends upon a respect of themselves, their classmates—and of her. She makes clear her expectations for excellent work and for proper behavior.

She spends time, as well, to process what learning means, which includes listening well, studying hard, cooperating with others, and bringing their best selves into the classroom every day. Inside the rigor of hard work, she lets students know that she cares about who they are and who they want to become.

Now that you've become a veteran teacher in your school, Pamela, I would be interested in your recollections of our workshops—and of my reflections in this letter. I remember you as a mature, clear-headed young teacher who made an impact on your students from your earliest days. I hope that when we discussed good classroom management you had the wisdom to realize that it was in support of strong relationships with all of your students. At least I hope that somehow I had made that clear.

I hope to hear from you soon.
Sincerely,
Fritz

POINTS TO PURSUE

Orienting new teachers

New teachers struggle with balancing what they want to accomplish and their need to maintain an orderly classroom. Some labor, while others seem more at ease. As in learning to ride a bicycle, once learned, you cannot tell who struggled more in the process.

What do you remember most about forming student relationships in your first year? Did you achieve a proper balance with your classroom management approach?

What can you do to help new teachers find this balance? What is your responsibility to help new teachers, particularly if you are not a mentor?

Intrinsic versus extrinsic classroom management

Every day teachers face the question of whether to exert extrinsic controls in the classroom or to trust intrinsic means. A student bursts out with an angry remark; another jumps out of his seat; another leans to whisper to a friend. In each instance, a teacher must decide how to respond.

Young teachers often choose extrinsic actions to restore order ("go to the office"; "sit down or you'll have detention"). The danger, however, is that extrinsic options can become routine and threaten the possibility of developing a warm tone.

If you tend to react quickly and firmly, how can you resist the temptation to control and instead to choose intrinsic options (i.e., to act as a mentor rather than enforcer)? A difficult question that demands thoughtful consideration.

Beyond the classroom

This letter advocates that teachers continue relationship building outside the classroom, both at school and beyond. Some teachers, however, make it a point to separate their private life and live in other communities.

What do you do beyond the classroom with students? How do you maintain a balance between your public and private life?

Your reputation precedes you

Teachers earn a reputation whether they are aware of it or not. Do you know your reputation in your school? How can you find out? How much do you think your reputation counts? Should you bother to pay attention to it?

Letters as social media

One final Point to Pursue: In these days of social media, assess the impact of letter writing. Draft one to a colleague, to an administrator, to a parent, or to your students, and see what transpires. You (and they) might be surprised.

Establish a dialogue with other teachers with your ideas. Log on to Teachingthatmatters.wordpress.com and join the conversation.

V

Build Trust and Respect

> Trust is like love. Both parties have to feel it before it really exists.
> —Simon Sinek

The decision to make trust and respect the centerpiece of schools makes it possible for all students to succeed.

In the conclusion to his provocative and intriguing book *How We Decide*, Jonah Lehrer shares how the aviation industry has practically eliminated pilot error.[1] First, Lehrer relates how pilots take flight simulation training to encounter scenarios that threaten safe flights. These sessions engage their emotions as well as their minds and prepare them to react without thinking. No more listening to lectures.

Second, pilots are trained in Cockpit Resource Management (CRM). It teaches them how during a crisis to seek and accept a diversity of viewpoints. Instead of expecting the captain to have "God-like certainty," everyone in the cockpit is instructed to say what he thinks.

Lehrer adds that surgical teams in hospitals have instituted CRM, notably the Nebraska Medical Center. Using its mantra, "See it, say it, fix it," surgical teams have tripled the number of "uneventful cases," where nothing has gone wrong during an operation.

He describes the pilot of the plane as its rational brain and the cockpit computers as its emotional brain. Both are necessary for successful flights. His description recalls Jonathan Haidt's metaphor of the rider and the elephant. In each person, Haidt describes, the rider—the mind or rational brain—looks out for possibilities while the elephant—the body or emotional brain—does what it's been trained to do.[2]

What might Lehrer's description of re-training pilots and surgeons have to do with schools?

Teachers work alone in their classrooms within a strict hierarchical, factory-model culture. They are positioned just above paraprofessionals, secretaries, janitors, and kitchen help. Authorities at the federal and state levels, school boards, superintendents, and principals determine most of what is to be taught and when—and take control of year-end assessment tests. In this framework, teachers are purveyors.

Lehrer's explanation of the process to eliminate pilot error suggests a new paradigm for schools. What if teachers participate in a CRM-like structure, in which they are included as equals at the decision-making table? What if "See it, say it, fix it" becomes embedded in school cultures, where teachers speak freely about school matters without fear of having to look over their shoulders? What if the culture of clout where higher-ups exert power becomes replaced by a democratic culture of mutual respect where everyone is listened to?

Would student learning improve under this new paradigm? Yes, only if school systems decide to make fundamental changes in the structure of schools as suggested in the above questions. They could begin by developing a "teaching-simulator" concept as part of teacher training—and for retraining (recertification) as well. This approach would replace the largely lecture-based preparation that is combined with six-to-nine weeks of practice teaching.[3] This concept can also be applied to professional development and education conferences that are traditionally lecture-driven.

Schools could choose to initiate School Resource Management (SRM) that would hear from all parties. Instead of administrators acting as decision makers, everyone learns how to have a say. "See it, say it, fix it" becomes a mantra that frees everyone to say what is necessary to make it possible for every student to succeed.

If this model is to work, teacher training needs to become more rigorous inside school settings. Following the medical-profession model, teachers would begin their careers as interns. While they do not require as many years of preparation as doctors (the expertise is not as precise), they should have more than they now receive.

Teachers need opportunities to work alongside master teachers and spend time observing in multiple classrooms, which approximates the grand-round process in hospitals. They should write frequently and reflect on their observations. As they develop and teach lessons, they need constant feedback from master teachers and peers. And they should meet frequently for reflection and discussion.

Once they receive a full-time contract, teachers should be assigned mentors who will shepherd them through their first three years. Having a mentor assures them of acquiring a deeper understanding of how the school operates including scheduling issues, report periods, discipline of students, and evaluations.

The rigor of this program makes it possible to raise the level of the teaching profession. Candidates who traditionally see entrance into the profession as a relatively easy path to employment will begin to understand the amount of time and expertise necessary before taking full responsibility for the classroom. The training, internship, and close scrutiny of the candidate process will raise the bar for becoming a teacher. It will attract higher-level candidates and bring more respect to the profession. This process will take time.

At present, entering teachers are barely prepared, yet they are expected to teach a full load from the first day. No wonder half of them leave within five years. Until society chooses to treat teaching as a valued profession and invest wisely in its future practitioners, "pilot error" in the profession will not be corrected anytime soon.

NOTES

1. Jonas Lehrer, *How We Decide* (New York: Mariner Books, 2009), "Coda," 251–59.
2. Jonathan Haidt, *The Happiness Hypothesis:Finding Modern Truth in Ancient Wisdom* (New York: Basic Books, 2006).
3. Notable exceptions are programs, such as the Upper Valley Educators Institute (UVEI) in Lebanon NH; the Teacher Training Course (TTC) at Shady Hill in Cambridge MA; the New Teachers Collaborative at the Francis W. Parker School in Devens MA., and the Newton Public Schools' Teacher Residency Program in Newton MA.

EIGHTEEN
Replace Factory Model Schools: Eliminate Debilitating Hierarchies

The lingering inertia of the factory-model school structure in America prompts important questions for the future of schools.

We are already into the second decade of the twenty-first century, yet schools act as if they intend to immortalize their factory-model origins. Despite the influx of SMART Boards, computers, cell phones, and iPads, a majority of students still sit with textbooks at desks in rows in front of teachers, just like generations before them. Bells ring to signal the start and end of periods and yellow buses deliver children from home to school and back.

So how did it all begin? From a conspiracy point of view, the scenario opens early in the last century. Leading industrial magnates are sitting in a back room around a conference table invoking the spirit of Frederick Winslow Taylor.[1] One of them offers a proposal:

> Why don't we set up schools to prepare citizens to work in factories? We will design the buildings to mirror assembly lines. We'll make long straight hallways with rooms on each side. Each room will have children's desks set in rows and columns. We'll place the teacher's desk in front with a blackboard behind.
>
> As we do in industry, we'll build the system from the top down. We'll hire men to be superintendents to organize each school and each classroom. They, in turn, will hire other men to be principals to oversee each building. The principals, then, will hire women as cheap labor to be teachers and place one in each room where they will carry out the superintendent's plans.
>
> The children will be assigned to grades based on their age. For each grade the superintendent will determine the curriculum, textbooks,

and the sequence of lesson plans. Teachers, in turn, will deliver these lessons and ask students to memorize and regurgitate the material. Each room will have a door with a clear glass panel to enable the principal to check on teachers.

We will require every child to attend public school, except for those whose families can afford to send their children to private institutions that we endow. Public schools will select the best students to attend college or to train for professions, such as medicine and law. Those children whose families have means can pursue business interests. The rest we will prepare to work in our factories.

The focus of public schools will be to prepare children for the workforce. They will learn to accept authority, follow instructions, complete repetitive tasks, and know their place in society. They will be indoctrinated in the American way: loyalty first to factory, then to their family, to the community, and finally to the nation.

This hierarchical factory-model system remained in place throughout the twentieth century and now into the early twenty-first century. Efforts at educational reform to break its rigid format have hardly made a dent. John Dewey and his Progressive Education colleagues, from the late nineteenth century to the mid-twentieth century, achieved some impact on educational practice. It was not, however, enough to subvert the factory-model system.

The Open Education movement in the 1970s, which grew out of England's Progressive Primary School movement, thrived briefly, but it also succumbed to the hierarchical structure of public schools.

A Nation at Risk, the 1983 report of President Reagan's National Commission on Excellence in Education, could be interpreted as an extension of hierarchical control of schools with its appeals for change. George W. Bush's No Child Left Behind and, perhaps less so, Arne Duncan's Race to the Top, also emulate the tradition of top-down control over schools, children, and families.

Today the Feds dangle funds in front of state and local authorities who are invited to comply or be resigned to an empty cupboard. The underlying criteria for these federal programs—and similar programs at the state level—rely on outside assessments that largely determine the success or failure of schools, students, and most recently teachers.

How, then, can this hierarchical paradigm be overturned and, in its place, be established a new focus on making successful learning possible for all students in all schools? It can begin in the mind of each teacher.

Imagine the following scenario: A teacher takes time before the first day of school and imagines herself standing at her classroom door at the *end* of the school year. She visualizes each of her incoming students leaving her classroom on their last day. She asks herself, "What will these students have learned because they have spent a year in my classroom?" She recalls some of the questions she asked about last year's students:

What does Isabel know about herself that she didn't know before arriving to my class?

Now, how well does Angela respect her peers, and how well do her peers respect her?

Is Tommy a more confident and motivated learner than when the year began?

How well does Ting exert leadership? How well does she follow?

What skills has Molly developed that will allow her to learn in future classrooms—and more importantly to learn on her own?

How is Jesse able to respond to surprises, new ways of how to think, imagine, and work? What still gets in his way?

What difficulties has Misha faced in her family and how has she responded? What support will she need?

How well has James integrated his interconnectivity-technology skills with face-to-face talking and sharing?

These questions are but a sample that swirls about in a teacher's mind. Together they indicate the deep complexity of the classroom and respect for the challenging work teachers do every day. The most important issues focus on intangibles and not on test outcomes.

What a shame that teachers feel pressure to comply with directives from authorities who determine the success or failure of their teaching—and many of them have never taught or have left the classroom so long ago that they've forgotten what it takes for teachers to succeed.

Successful teaching comes from years of responding to the above questions—and countless more. Ask any teacher about a former student and she will talk about who she is, not about her test scores, if she even remembers them. Ask her, too, if would she have decided to become a teacher if she had known that she would have to teach her students how take multiple-choice bubble-tests and that these tests would determine her success?

In Jonathan Haidt's rider/elephant metaphor cited earlier, the rider represents our mind that looks around and conjures possibilities, sometimes exciting us to the point that we think we will immediately implement them. The elephant, on the contrary, reflects our habitual responses, what we've learned to do automatically to sustain our daily lives.

We often underestimate the strength of our elephant. When, for instance, we see a film, such as Frederick Wiseman's *Meat*, that shames us into not eating beef, our rider swears to stop our habit. Three weeks later, our elephant has us eating barbecued hamburgers.

Annual outside assessments assume that students and teachers are like Haidt's riders. Teachers are told to deliver information that students are expected to absorb and then take tests to verify (usually on Fridays). Such testing assesses quick learning, often through memorization. Yet real learning, as represented by Haidt's elephant, takes time and persistence. To learn worthwhile knowledge, understanding, and skills requires commitment and practice. It includes asking questions and teaching students to ask questions, a skill that's rarely taught.

When authorities ask teachers to teach to multiple-choice bubble-tests, they deprive them and their students of the potential joy of discovering insights that emerge from thoughtful considerations. Students are shortchanged when they think that the quicker they "get it" the smarter they are, when those smarts are often ethereal at best. When knowledge is memorized for tests, it is often forgotten soon after.

When tests become the sole assessment criteria for success, teachers do not contemplate the impact of their teaching. Unlike the teacher who reflects about questions for each of her students at the end of the year, a test-driven teacher simply stands at her door and sees students leaving with labels stuck on their foreheads. These labels indicate scores from several days—in some cases weeks—of sitting and filling in bubble after bubble after bubble.

Good teachers train the elephant. They engage in teaching habits of mind that serve the greater good of each person and society. They invite students to accept challenges and give support along the way. They encourage them to be prepared for an unknown future. And they seek answers to questions they ask about each child throughout the year.

It's time to declare that teaching and learning is not a business, that it does not seek to make a profit and construct a successful balance sheet. It is personal. It's about patience and persistence. It's about supporting students to become who they are meant to become and about how they can be of service to others.

If students are only taught to regurgitate memorized moments, write formulaic five-paragraph essays, answer repetitive math questions, and repeat memorized clauses of the U.S. Constitution, learning will, as my colleague Frank Gould says, "be like spitballs that cling to the wall without meaning." Students will not acquire the necessary knowledge and skills to do a job.[2]

And when people understand that the tyranny of outside assessments is determining the fate of our schools, they should certainly consider the possibility of the corporate conspiracy that established the first factory-model schools. Until then, they can invoke the words of Phillip Pullman:

> We should [not] give up and surrender. . . . I think we should act *as if*. I think we should read books, and tell children's stories, and take them to the theatre, and learn poems, and play music, as if it would make a difference. . . . We should act as if the universe were listening to us and responding. We should act as if we were going to win.[3]

NOTES

1. http://en.wikipedia.org/wiki/Frederick_Winslow_Taylor.
2. Personal correspondence.
3. Laura Miller, "Far From Narnia: Philip Pullman's Secular Fantasy for Children,"
3.

NINETEEN

Invoke a New Paradigm: Make Trust and Respect the Centerpiece of Schools

When all parties have the courage to trust each other, they make it possible for schools to become the democratic institutions they need to be.

For at least the past twenty years, education policy makers have declared that the benchmark of school success should be based on what students *learn*, not on what teachers *teach*. In Massachusetts, for example, the State Department of Education's Massachusetts Comprehensive Assessment System (MCAS) exam has become the major determiner of student and school success. The test and practice tests take up five to six weeks of class time a year. And such exams are now a significant factor in evaluating teacher competency, as well.

These year-end tests can deny teachers and students time to pursue ambiguities, ponder perplexing problems, think about thinking, discuss pressing matters, and engage in important tangential conversations. Pressure to prepare for tests can smother the possibility of creating a unique classroom dynamic.

Despite contrary pronouncements by policy makers, teaching for success on multiple-choice bubble-tests demands bubble teaching. It means skipping from one thing to another to another. No time for lingering. No time for immersion. No time for thinking. No time for relationships.

Meanwhile, schools perpetuate a fiefdom mindset, a self-driven, embedded isolated world that protects them from outsiders. Teachers hunker down in their private classrooms behind closed doors. Principals hole up in their offices, as they try to keep up with paperwork and endless mini-crises. Secretaries set up domains difficult to penetrate. Parents often feel intimidated when they come into schools; they may have had bad encounters as students, or they may fear being seen as inferior to teachers. Students feel isolated, too, as arbitrary schedules and rigid rules keep them separated from friends.[1]

The fiefdom mentality also exists between principal and teachers. In many schools, principals are only allowed restricted access to classrooms. Many teachers feel that they have a natural right to decide who comes into their rooms, whether this provision is in the union contract or not—an ironic right to privacy in schools that are publicly funded.

Consultants feel this fiefdom mentality, too. Once when Fritz Thomas was teaching a course on pedagogy to teachers, the superintendent asked him to visit classrooms to provide feedback on the strategies discussed. When Bill, an entrenched teacher who distrusted the administration, declared that he did not want Fritz to visit his classroom, no one questioned his right; it was, after all, his fiefdom.

A week later, Fritz took a chance and stopped by during a recess and gently scaled the walls of Bill's castle and was "allowed" to stay through a couple of lessons.

As long as schools perpetuate the fiefdom culture, all parties—central office, principals, teachers, specialists, and parents—become susceptible to blame when matters take a downturn. Playing the blame game creates openings for critics-of-the-moment to step in and declare that they know the causes of the failure and how to fix it. When new failures become evident (as they inevitably do), other critics seize the moment, establish their credentials, and set the cycle in motion again. Hence, efforts to reform succumb to pontifications, rather than making real change.

Instead of pontifications, administrators and teachers need to ask themselves:

- How will we break out of this embedded fiefdom culture?
- How will we make the natural richness of teaching and learning become the centerpiece of education?
- How will we become free to create and develop dynamic, exciting, enriching learning communities?
- And, how will our schools and classrooms become about the students first?

The answer to these questions lies in what, upon reflection, should be obvious: *All parties in schools must commit to building a democratic framework of mutual respect and trust.* This commitment means hard work for everyone. Unlike mandated testing programs, trust cannot be imposed but has to be grown.

As giving cannot happen without receiving, so it is true with trust. Trust becomes mutual when reciprocated. Once having trust, people want to be worthy of it. Building trust inside hierarchical schools will take unwavering persistence and commitment from everyone. Such a democratic paradigm change may appear impossible on the surface, but like great changes throughout history, it can begin anywhere and at any time with a few determined people.

Teachers take initiative. Teachers do not have to wait for someone to tell them to change practice. For example, a teacher recognizes that her students' persistent inattention hinders her lessons. She decides to look for better ways to connect with them. She opens her door to a colleague to receive feedback. In turn, the two of them encourage others to open their doors.

Making such a significant trust transition takes time, as the habit of teaching alone resides deep in teachers' psyches. Those who choose to collaborate soon discover that they learn more about teaching and become better able to respond to their students.[2]

Teachers become receptive to new ideas and methodologies. Young children learn embedded habits of teaching from kindergarten. By fourth grade they internalize how to succeed. To break this entrenched cycle, a teacher does not put on blinders, nor does she ignore the new demands of today's society.

Instead, she lets go of outmoded traditional habits and becomes open to new approaches. She recognizes that the present fast-moving culture requires that she create and invent ways to meet her digitally dependent students more than halfway if necessary.

Professional Development becomes integral to the school day. Teachers and administrators need professional development, as do all professionals. Traditionally scheduled only for two or three days a year, professional development should be integrated into the school's schedule.

Given that the pace of potential change happens faster than ever, educators need consistent retraining to better meet today's digitally dependent students. They need consistent opportunities for collaboration. And they should decide for themselves the professional development that they need.

Teachers open their classrooms to administrators. Teachers have managed to keep administrators at bay except for the required annual—and often unproductive—dog-and-pony visits. Yet they need supportive feedback from both administrators and colleagues. They can choose to invite principals to observe everyday classroom activities even if it requires training them what to look for. Such a change in mindset takes patience from both parties.

Professional Learning Communities (PLCs) bring teachers and administrators together to meet regularly to collaborate on ways to improve teaching and learning.[3]

Teachers elect principals. One of the fixtures in the hierarchy of schools is the appointment of principals to govern faculties. This act alone separates a principal from teachers and defines the potential for animosity between them. When teachers elect a leader, however, both have a vested interest in each other. Trust and mutual respect form the basis of the relationship.[4]

Principals acknowledge teachers as primary decision makers. Effective leadership means that principals recognize teachers as the primary decision makers in their classrooms. They agree to work alongside them and their students—and equally important, encourage collaboration throughout the school.[5] Central office administration, too, must publicly recognize teachers as primary decision makers and support principals in their effort to work with teachers.

Students, after all, deserve to have competent teachers who make it possible to realize their potential every day. It's not fair to put parents and students in the position of having to advocate for particular teachers who they perceive are "the good ones" or to try to avoid those they think are "bad."

Personnel evaluations can be and should be peer based. Traditionally, superintendents evaluate principals, principals evaluate teachers, and teachers evaluate paraprofessionals. Inside a democratic paradigm of trust, however, evaluations can come from where they best serve the persons being evaluated.

Teachers can evaluate each other, as well as evaluate administrators. Principals can evaluate one another as well as central office personnel. Principals can still continue to evaluate teachers but more from the point of view of colleagues who partner, rather than as authorities who threaten.

Teachers initiate trust relationships with students. Teachers can shift from seeing students as receptacles of knowledge to seeing them as learning partners. Once a teacher affirms this trust—which takes time and patience—students become freer to engage. They learn to value partnering with the teacher and their fellow students. They learn, too, to accept struggle as an essential ingredient for learning. They become decision makers who realize the value of work and of being willing to work. Cooperation, not competition, becomes the watchword.

Teachers understand that all students are the responsibility of every teacher. In a democratic paradigm, no longer are teachers left alone to deal with difficult students. Instead every teacher in the subject, grade, and team—and throughout the school—has a shared responsibility for these students—and these students know that every teacher cares for them.[6] Such open collaboration builds mutual respect among teachers and with students.

Test results belong to everyone. Because every teacher focuses on students' learning potential, students who struggle do not hold back everyone else's progress. They no longer remain hidden behind the closed doors of isolated classrooms and viewed as products of bad teachers.

Successful students who do well on tests are not ignored either. Instead, schools and teachers find ways to develop the full potential of every one of their students. Excellent test scores and poor test scores belong to everyone.

All parties listen to one another. Listening begets listening. Administrators listen to teachers without making judgments. Teachers listen to administrators without making assumptions. Teachers listen to students without interrupting.

Imagine a school where people pay attention to each other as they do to a movie on the big screen. Alive with listening, classrooms become open to everyone's ideas. And so, too, with listening throughout the school.[7]

Implementing a paradigm shift in schools that is built on trust and respect is daunting. Given the embedded hierarchical structure of schools, some might argue that it's impossible. But it is essential if schools are to become twenty-first century learning institutions in which all students have opportunities to develop competencies for success.

This process begins with developing trust in teachers—a trust that is acknowledged outright. With nonjudgmental support, teachers become free to do their best without having to look over their shoulder for rebuke or approval.

Inside this democratic paradigm, new initiatives raise expectations and assure greater excellence. No more covering up for teachers who hang onto their classrooms until retirement. No more proficient and exemplary evaluations of 90 percent of teachers in schools where half the students are failing.[8] Trust allows for full transparency throughout the school. Together, everyone strives for excellence.

The ideas offered here are but a beginning. When administrators and faculty choose to move into a democratic paradigm where all parties have equal say, they will discover other ideas and approaches. Schools, like individuals, have their own personalities, their own cultures. Together staff, students, and parents can create democratic solutions that provide opportunities for everyone to succeed.

Ultimately, when schools fail to develop a democratically based system of mutual trust and respect among all parties, including students, they will likely fall further into the sinkhole of having to strive for compliance to multiple-choice bubble-tests that sort, select, and deny. Schools cannot afford, however, to waste anyone. Nor is it morally right.

NOTES

1. Michael Schmoker articulates a "buffer-zone" concept for schools that led me to describe the fiefdom domains. (See Michael Schmoker, *Results Now*, chapter 1, "The Buffer," 13–22.) I want to thank Chet Kozwolski for coming up with the term *fiefdom*, which he saw as directly describing what I have written.

2. Carrie Leana, "The Missing Link in School Reform?" *Stanford Social Innovation Review* (Fall 2011) from *Teacher*, Sept. 1, 2011 cited in The Marshall Memo 402, September 19, 2011. The article stresses the importance of teachers as social capital over human capital, http://www.ssireview.org/articles/entry/the_missing_link_in_school_reform/.

3. The Professional Learning Community reform effort led by Richard and Rebecca DuFour has demonstrated an effective way for teachers and administrators to work together to focus on students learning. Solution Tree is the best resource at: http://www.solution-tree.com/Public/Main.aspx.

4. Donaldo Macedo pointed out this fact in "Beyond a Domesticating Education: A Dialogue" in a conversation with Noam Chomsky in his edited book *Chomsky on MisEducation* (Lanham, MD: Rowman & Littlefield, 2000), 27. I am baffled that I never thought of this idea myself.

5. Carrie Leana, "The Missing Link in School Reform?"

6. Vivian Troen of Brandeis shared this idea at "Special WBUR Event: Is Good Teaching Teachable?" from WBUR studios, May 26, 2011: http://www.wbur.org/2011/05/26/live-teaching-discussion.

7. For a lucid description of the power of listening, see Rebecca Z. Shafir, *The Zen of Listening: Mindful Communication in the Age of Distraction* (Wheaton, IL: Quest Books, 2000), chapter 5, "What's Their Movie?" 81–102.

8. Meg Campbell, "Grade inflation for Boston teachers?" *Boston Globe*, May 24, 2013. Meg Campbell points out the discrepancy that 92 percent of Boston teachers who were evaluated received proficient or exemplary ratings, while more than 50 percent of Boston students were failing.

Epilogue

Having schools in which all parties trust and respect one another is a high ideal but one that every school community can strive for. Until teachers become central in the decision-making process, they are vulnerable to criticism whenever anything goes wrong. Such blame leads to defensiveness and to more blame.

In a democratic culture of trust, all parties work together toward solutions. When wrongs appear, as they inevitably do, everyone pitches in to fix them. Mutual respect requires commitment from everyone, from the superintendent to the maintenance staff. And, it includes students.

Teachers, secretaries, paraprofessionals, guidance counselors, principals and assistant principals, deans, nurses, et al. serve to make a school function. Teachers, for their part, need to respect the janitors who clean their classrooms, the cooks who prepare their food, the administrators who support them, and the students who sit before them. Without them, they would be unable to teach.

Understanding the dignity of each person opens the door to removing the hierarchical structure of schools and replacing it with a democratically based system of mutual trust and respect.

Index

ADD, 52
administrators: fear of being watched by, 13; letter to, 10, 11, 12; opening classrooms to, 165; open office doors of, 13; teacher relationships with, 9–13
adolescent recruitability, 72
Alicia, consultant's letter to, 135–139
always do your best, as fourth agreement, 129–130
ambiguity: invoking, 26; lesson plans, 21–27; 10-2 method for creating, 22–24, 26
American Idol, 90
Amur, Musad, 22–25, 26
analogies: frog, 52, 59; symphony, 63, 65
ancient history, as curriculum change example, 96–98
Animal Farm (Orwell), xx
Anthony, Carol, 107
apathy, in students, 52
Apple, 82, 83–85, 115, 116
arts in education, 43–44; brain research on, 44; decrease in, 44; teacher conundrum, 48
assessment: curriculum additions for sake of, 121; formative, 10; MCAS, 163; summative, 10. *See also* evaluations; tests and testing
assumptions: common practice of making, 131; in four agreements, 128; ignition key example of making, 103, 105; teacher, 103–104, 128
attention spans, 36
"At the Center" (Norris, M.), 95–96

babies, deprived of human contact, 72
Backward Design, 54–55, 59, 106

being in moment, 56
beliefs, teacher's personal, 131
Berry, Thomas, 65, 66, 67, 69, 96
Beyond War, 96
Bhagavad Gita, 129
big bang, 96, 97
blogs, 57, 91, 92
books: book group, 43, 45; value of, 40
Boston Globe, 115
brain research, 39–48; on arts in education, 44; on physical exercise, 41–42, 47, 49n7; on sleep, 42–43
Brain Rules (Medina), 40, 41–43
Brain-Targeted Teaching Model for 21st Century, 45–46, 48, 49n14
Bramble, Dennis, 64
Brentwood, Allison, 77–81
Brooks, Walter, 125–130, 131
Buddha, 56
Budd Rowe, Mary, xxivn4, 22
bullying, 73
Bush, George W., 158
bus metaphor, 78–79, 81
butterfly, 121–122
bystander metaphor, 100–102

Cain, Susan, 13n2
Camden, Joe, 66–67, 69
Campbell Murphy, Elspeth, 46, 128
cards: Exit, 18; Recap, 18; ticket-to-leave, 45
Carlton, Pat, 15
Carr, Nicholas, 56
Carrier, David, 64
Carroll, James, 115
Catcher in the Rye (Salinger), 53–54
cave paintings, 63
cell phones, 55, 87
CFGs. *See* Critical Friends Groups
chaos, 125

Chauvet, France, 63
chefs, gladiator, 100
Child, Julia, 90, 91
Chinese history course, 96, 97, 98
Chinese philosophy class, 77–78
classrooms: beyond, 150; expanding reach of, 91, 92; intrinsic *vs.* extrinsic management of, 150; isolated, 3–8, 80, 90, 92; open-door, 12–13, 165; personal beliefs and, 131; as private worlds, 7, 90, 92; teacher impact on safe, 46; teaching from front of, xxii; well-managed, 148–149
clickers, 18
coaching, 15–18. *See also* feedback; mentor-protégé relationships
Cockpit Resource Management (CRM), 153
The Cognitive Style of PowerPoint: Pitching Out Corrupts Within (Tufte), 115, 117
collegiality, 37, 143, 144
Columbia space shuttle, 115
community issues, writing about, 91
composure, 122, 124
confidentiality: classroom isolation and, 4–8; consideration of, 7; mentor-protégé, 3–4
Confucius, 77–78, 97, 130
congeniality, 143, 144
consultants: fiefdom mindset felt by, 164; letters to new teachers from, 135–139, 141–145, 147–151; teacher feedback from, 15–17. *See also* coaching
Contact (Sagan), 98
conversations, 29–37; digital culture lessening of, 35–36; in human history, 33; Inside-Outside Circles for, 32; Internet impact on, 34; Internet Sabbaths for improving, 55, 60; inventing images in, 33, 37n6; messiness in, 34; valuing, 29–34
cooking, 90; reality show on, 100
Co-opoly game, xx
corporate control, of media, 112
Cosmos, 98
Cranbrook, Brett, 106–107

Critical Friends Groups (CFGs), 3, 5–6, 7–8
CRM. *See* Cockpit Resource Management
culture: biological *vs.* cultural evolution, 64; changing, 68, 144–145; cultural speed, 68; democratic paradigm and, 154, 166–168, 169; factory-model, 153; faculty room, 144; fiefdom, 163–164; hunter-gatherer, 63–64, 68. *See also* digital culture
curiosity, 31, 69
curriculum: changes and demands, 96–98, 121; teacher control of, 99

DeBono, Edward, 30, 36
delivery-style teaching, xxiii, 78, 79; from front of classroom, xxii; letter on, 141–143; persistence of, 143; slides as, 114. *See also* lecture style
democratic paradigm, 154, 166–168, 169
desired results, as UbD premise, 54, 106
Dewey, John, 158
Differentiated Instruction (DI), 53–54, 55, 59; website, 59
digital culture, 111, 114; actively responding to, 59–60; conversation lessening by, 35–36; electronic devices and, 51–52, 59–60
Dilbert (cartoon), 86–89
"Diplomacy" board game, xix–xx
discipline, 139
Disney, Walt, 112
distraction, electronic devices as causing, 52
dog-and-pony-show model, 11, 12
don't take anything personally, as second agreement, 127
The Dragons of Eden (Sagan), 98
Duncan, Arne, 158
Duncan, George, 119–120

education: IEPs, 90; Open Education movement, 158; Progressive Education, 158. *See also* physical education

Effinger, Joe, 63–64, 68
Einstein, Albert, 1
electronic devices: cell phones, 55, 87; digital culture and, 51–52, 59–60; distractions caused by, 52; human contact issue with, 56; in introverted student life example, 46, 51–52, 57; memory and, 51; time away from, 55
elephant metaphor, 153, 159–160
Ely, Elissa, 100, 101
emperor wearing no clothes, 111; PowerPoint as, 111, 113, 116
equality, as valuing conversation principle, 30
Escalante, Jaime, xxiii
essays, 76; on community issues, 91; handwritten, 84; to newspapers and blogs, 91; to other students, 91; revising, 82–85. *See also* letters
evaluations: personnel, 166; teacher, 167, 168n8
evidence, as UbD premise, 55, 106
evolution: biological *vs.* cultural, 64; human, 63–65, 68, 69
The Evolving Self (Kegan), 72, 73, 74
exercise, brain research on, 41–42, 47, 49n7
Exit Cards, 18

Facebook, 52, 57
face-to-face interaction, 114
facilitators, teachers as, 114, 117
factory-model schools, 153, 157–160
faculty, 7–8; collegiality, 37, 143, 144; engaging fellow, 37; faculty-room culture, 144
fame, 90
fear, 13
federal programs, 158
feedback, 103–104; active, 15; anonymous student, 18, 19n3; to loud-voiced teacher, 15–17; permission for offering, 17; positive, 17; on teacher assumptions, 128
fidgetiness, 87, 88–89
fiefdom culture, 163–164
Finland, 91
Fitzgerald, Carl, 73

Flanagan, Brian, 73
flatline time, 47
footprints, 97–98
force of one, 144–145
formative assessment, 10
four agreements: always do your best, 129–130; choosing to honor, 129; don't make assumptions, 128; impeccability, 126–127; not taking things personally, 127
The Four Agreements (Ruiz), 125–131
France, cave paintings in Chauvet, 63
frog analogy, 52, 59
Frost, Robert, 32
full-engagement paradigm, 66

Gabler, Neil, 60n1
Gandhi, Mohandas Karamchand, 111, 145
gladiator chefs, 100
Gonzalez, José, 44–45, 48
Google, 47, 52, 58, 96
Gould, Frank, 160
grades: apathy about, 52; grading papers without names, 104, 105; lecture style and, 26
gray kids, 72
Green, George, 56
Greenleaf, Robert, 46, 49n15
groups: CFG, 3, 5–6, 7–8; students choosing, 86–89; working alone or in, 87
grump factor, 40

Haidt, Jonathan, 153, 159–160
Haines, Mike, 91
Hamlet's Blackberry (Powers), 55
Hammond, Emily, 90–92
handwritten essays, 84
Hardiman, Mariale, 45–46, 48
Harris, Mark, 5, 6
hierarchical system, 164–168, 169
Higgs Boson, 55
Hillman, James, 37n6
history: conversation in human, 33; courses, 96, 97, 98; teaching ancient, 96–98
Homo sapiens. See Running Man

How the Brain Learns (National Research Council), 40
How the Brain Learns (Sousa), 40
How We Decide (Lehrer), 153
Hubble, Edward, 97
human contact: babies deprived of, 72; gift of, 56; Internet Sabbaths and, 60
human evolution, 63–65; cultural speed and, 68; future, 69
hunter-gatherer culture, 63–64, 68

I Ching, 107, 108
IEPs. *See* Individual Education Plans
ignition key incident, 103, 105
images, inventing, 33, 37n6
ImageWriter, 82
immersive attention, 123
impeccability, 126–127
Individual Education Plans (IEPs), 90
inequalities, recruitability and, 72, 74
innovation: impetus for, xxiii; resistance to, xxii; social studies example of, xix–xxi
Inside-Outside Circles, 32
insights, 75–76
Integrating Differentiated Instruction and Understanding by Design (Tomlinson and McTighe), 59
intentions: lesson plans and, 106–107; paper cutter plans and, 106, 107; planning while knowing, 106–107
Internet: conversation impact of, 34; impact of, xxii; omnicentricity, 98; Sabbaths, 55, 60, 85; as universe, 95–96, 98, 99. *See also* digital culture; Google; social media
introverts, 11, 13n2, 46, 51–52, 57, 142
inventing images, 33, 37n6
iPad, 84
isolation, classroom, 3–4, 80, 90, 92; confidentiality and, 4–8
Ivan IV, xx

Jenisch, Martin, 66, 67
Jensen, Eric, 40, 44–46
Jobs, Steve, xxiii, 115–116
Johansen, Sarah, 65–67
Johns Hopkins University, 45–46, 48, 49n14

Johnson, Betty, 90, 91
Julie and Julia, 90, 91

Khan Academy, xxii–xxiii
Kazantzakis, Nikos, 121–122, 123
Keenan, Edward L., xx
Kegan, Robert, 72, 73, 74
Keynote slides, 114, 116
Kurzweil, Ray, 68, 69

Lao Tzu, 97
Lawrence, Morton, 65, 66, 67
learning: PLCs, 165, 168n3; Primacy-Recency, 44–45
lecture style, 22, 141–143; grades and, 26; teacher training and, 154–155, 155; 10-2 method, xxii, xxivn4, 22–24, 26. *See also* delivery-style teaching
Lehrer, Jonah, 153
lesson plans: ambiguity in, 21–27; intentions and, 106–107; pacing in, 26; pressure to create perfect, 22; student participation in, 26; UbD, 54–55, 59, 106; unexpected input affecting, 25, 106–107
lessons: cell phones incorporated into, 55; open-ended, 21; problems with sticking to designed, 21–22; website posting of, 80. *See also* writing
letters: to administrator, 10, 11, 12; to newspapers and blogs, 91; to new teachers, 135–139, 141–145, 147–151; to other students, 91; on prioritizing relationships, 147–151; as social media, 150–151; student-teacher, 9–10, 12; value of writing, 133–134; Zander, 9–10, 12
Levy, Kathleen, 43–44
Liebenberg, Louis, 64, 68
listening, 29, 167; attention span building through, 36; as conversation principle, 31–33; repeating and, 32
Lockhart, Fran, 57
long-term memory: sleep and, 60; technology effect on, 56
Looking at Student Work: A Window into the Classroom, 5, 7–8

Macintosh computers, 82; macro keys, 82, 83–85
Mahoney, Tom, 21–22
mantra, Nhat Hanh's, 104, 105, 124
Markus, George, 10–11
Martin, Shirley, 5–6
Marxist-Communism, xix
Mason, Shelley, 86–89
Massachusetts Comprehensive Assessment System (MCAS), 163
Mastering the Art of French Cooking (Child), 90
math, xxi–xxii
MCAS. *See* Massachusetts Comprehensive Assessment System
McDougall, Christopher, 64
McGuinness, Marta, 30–36
McKibben, Bill, 97–98
McLean, Norman, 100–101
McMillan, Jim, xxi–xxiii
McTighe, Jay, 59
Meat, 159
media: corporate control of, 112; writing letters to, 91. *See also* social media
Medina, John, 40, 41–43
meditation, 100
Memento, 51, 58, 60n1
memory: electronic device impact on, 51; sleep and, 60; technology effect on, 56
mentor-protégé relationships, 5, 6, 7, 154; confidentiality of, 3–4; mentor workshop, 9–10; second mentors, 6
messiness, conversation, 34
metaphors: bus, 78–79, 81; bystander, 100–102; Internet-universe, 95–96, 98, 99; rider-elephant, 153, 159–160, 160
Milley, Bob, xxivn3
mindfulness, 104, 122
The Miracle of Mindfulness (Nhat Hanh), 104
Mongiello, Peg, 37n5
Morris, Winslow, 96
movie, living in own, 130–131
multiple-choice tests, 163
music teachers, 48

names: grading papers without, 104, 105; remembering students, 71–72, 73
naps, 42–43; power, 43, 47–48
National Research Council, 40
National School Reform Faculty, 7–8
A Nation at Risk, 158
NCLB. *See* No Child Left Behind
Nebraska Medical Center, 153
newspapers, 91
new teachers, 72–73; consultant letters to, 135–139, 141–145, 147–151; orienting, 149–150; recruitability conundrum of, 71–72, 73; struggles of, 139
New York Times, 90, 91
Nhat Hanh, Thich, 103, 104, 105, 124
99 percent emptiness concept, 97
No Child Left Behind (NCLB), 158
nonaction, countering stress with, 100–102
Norris, Jordan, 66
Norris, Mark, 95–98
Norton, Ann, 15–17
Novig, Peter, 115
Noyes, Bill, 144
NPR, 60

offices, administrator, 13
Olson, Fred, 82–85
omnicentricity, 97, 98
open-door classrooms, 12–13, 165
Open Education movement, 158
orientation, new teacher, 149–150
Orson, Marie, 9, 10–11
Orwell, George, xx
outcomes, plans as different from, 108
overheads, 113–114. *See also* PowerPoint

pacing, 26; teaching schedule and, 77
painter, 119–120
paintings: cave, 63; viewing assignment, 121, 123
Palmer, Jesse, 120
Pamela (former new teacher), consultant's letter to, 147–151
paper cutter incident, 106, 107
Patterson, Jesse, 80

peace, 125
Peck, Scott, 75
personal beliefs, 131
personal freedom, 127, 130
personnel evaluations, 166
person-to-person skills, social media as detracting from, 55
Peter (new teacher), consultant letter to, 141–145
Peters, Pam, 3–4, 9–10, 11
Peterson, Dan (language arts teacher), 52–58, 59
physical education, 41
physical exercise, brain research on, 41–42, 47, 49n7
pilot training, 153, 155
plans: IEPs, 90; intentions and, 106–107; outcomes as different from, 108; as UbD premise, 55, 106. *See also* lesson plans
PLCs. *See* Professional Learning Communities
positive feedback, 17
Powell, Julie, 90, 91
PowerMac, 82
power naps, 43, 47–48
PowerPoint, 115; assessing use of, 116–117; as delivery-focused teaching, 114; as emperor wearing no clothes, 111, 113, 116; limitations of, 115–116; packets replacing, 114; printed page *vs.*, 117; Rosling's use of, 116, 117–118; TED talk use of, 116, 117–118
Powers, William, 55
presenters, teachers as facilitators or, 114, 117
present moment living, 56, 58
Primacy-Recency, 44–45; website, 49n13
principals, teacher election of, 166
prodding, 123
professional development, 165
Professional Learning Communities (PLCs), 165, 168n3
Progressive Education, 158
Pullman, Phillip, 160
Pythagorean Theorem, 45

questions, asking big, 68–69
quotations, in DI, 54

Race to the Top (RTTT), 101, 158
Reagan, Ronald, 158
reality show, on cooking, 100
Recap Cards, 18
recipes, in DI, 54
recruitability, 71–74; adolescent, 72; new teacher conundrum of, 71–72, 73
reflection, conversation principle of, 33–34
relationships: prioritizing teacher-student, 147–151; teacher-administrator, 9–13. *See also* mentor-protégé relationships
repeating, listening and, 32
research: avoiding shoddy, 39; web site searching and, 47. *See also* brain research
Reynolds, Joe, 136
rider-elephant metaphor, 153, 159–160, 160
Rilke, Rainer Maria, 29
Robert, Jennifer L., 121
Roberto (painter), 119–120
Roberts, Jennifer, 123
Robinson, John, 103–104
Rodgers, Phil, 15–17, 105; ignition key incident, 103, 105
Rodriguez, Ann, 5–6
Rosling, George Hans, 116, 117–118
Ross, Paul, 42–43, 47
RTTT. *See* Race to the Top
Ruiz, Don Miguel, 125–131
Running Man (Homo sapiens), 64
Russian history course, 96, 98. *See also* Soviet Union

Sabbaths, Internet, 55, 60, 85
safety: classroom, 46; recruitability for school, 71–74
Sagan, Carl, 67, 96, 98
Salinger, J. D., 53–54
schedule, pacing and, 77
School Resource Management (SRM), 154
selfishness, 127

Senge, Peter, 37n2
Shadows of Our Forgotten Ancestors (Sagan), 98
The Shallows (Carr), 56
simulation: flight, 153; in teacher training, 154
Sinek, Simon, 153
singularity, Kurzweil's, 68, 69
Six Hat Thinking (DeBono), 30, 36
Skype, 91
sleep: deprivation, 57; long-term memory and, 60; Medina's brain rule on, 42–43
slides. *See* overheads; PowerPoint
SMART board, xxi, 55, 79–80
social media, xxi, 52, 57; crisis resulting from, 57; interpersonal skills diminished by, 55; letters as, 150–151; present moment living due to, 56, 58; teacher use of, 55
social studies, innovation example and, xix–xxi
Socrates, 67
Sorenson, Alice, 71, 73
Sousa, David, 40, 44
Soviet Union, xx
speed, 119–124; butterfly hatching, 121–122; cultural, 68; of each student, 120, 122–123; painter example of natural, 119–120; universe at own, 123
SRM. *See* School Resource Management
Stand and Deliver, xxiii
standing still, 101
stress, nonaction technique for countering, 100–102
students: accepting without prejudging, 36; anonymous feedback from, 18, 19n3; apathy in, 52; baffling nature of today's, 58–59; complex lives of, xxi; conversations lacking in today's, 35–36; decision-making by teachers and, 88, 89; DI initial response of, 54; Dilbert example of giving choices to, 86–89; empathizing with, 140; expanding worldviews of, 90–92; favorite, 73; fidgety, 87, 88–89; Finland, 91;

Google use by, 52, 58; gray, 72; group size choosing by, 86–89; introvert, 11, 13n2, 46, 51–52, 57, 142; learning names of, 71–72, 73; lesson plan participation of, 26; letters to teachers from, 9–10, 12; meeting on own terms, 85; noting differences of today's, 139; prioritizing relationships with, 147–151; recruitability of all, 71–72, 73; revisions resisted by, 83; sleep deprivation in, 57; speed of each, 120, 122–123; teacher initiation of trust relations with, 166; teacher responsibility for, 166–167; unexpected input from, 106–107; unfolding of, 123; ways of engaging, 137; working alone or in groups, 87; writing essays to fellow, 91
summative assessment, 10
Sweller, Jonathan, 56
Swimme, Brian, 65, 66, 67, 69, 96
symphony, teaching to whole: analogy, 63, 65–67; asking big questions for, 68–69; testing as challenge to, 65–67, 69

tablets, 84
Tarahumara Indians, 64, 67
Taylor, Frederick Winslow, 157
T-charts, 53
teachers: administrators and, 9–13; art and music, 48; assumptions made by, 103–104, 128; classroom safety and, 46; collegiality among, 37, 143, 144; curriculum changes demanded of, 96–98; curriculum control of, 99; decision-making by students and, 88, 89; decision to become, 39; discipline help for, 139; drop-out percentage among, 7; evaluations of, 167, 168n8; as facilitators or presenters, 114, 117; fear of being watched in, 13; feedback to loud-voiced, 15–17; Google challenges for, 52, 58; initiative-taking by, 165; innovative, xix–xxi, xxii, xxiii; letters from students to, 9–10, 12; letters to new, 135–139, 141–145,

147–151; personal beliefs of, 131; as primary decision makers, 166; principals elected by, 166; professional development for, 165; questions asked by, 158–159; receptivity to new methodologies, 165; reputations of, 150; social media use by, 55; status-quo behavior in, 40; struggles of, 137, 139, 140n2; student responsibility of, 166–167; trust in, 79, 99; trust relations with students initiated by, 166; uniqueness of each, 140; young, 25. *See also* new teachers

teacher training, 154–155; simulation use in, 154

teaching: as act of love, 128; celebrating, 139; complexity of, xix; delivery-style, xxii, xxiii, 78, 79, 114, 141–143; demands on, 39; as discovery, 95; factory-model, 153, 157–160; from front of classroom, xxii; as profession, 135–136; re-imagining, 1–2; schedule and pacing dilemma in, 77; successful, 159; as time-clock job, 142; traditional, xxi–xxii, 11, 143

technology: essay writing and revisions with, 82–85; long-term memory impacted by, 56; macro keys and, 82, 83–85; slides and, 116; tablets and, 84

TED talks, 116, 117–118

10-2 method, xxii, xxivn4, 22–24, 26

tests and testing, 101, 160; limits of, 69; multiple-choice, 163; narrow focus on, 65–67; results ownership, 167; symphony analogy and, 65–67, 69; teaching/not teaching to, 78–79, 81

textbook elimination, xxii

"think-I-know-best" mindset, 103

Thomas, Fritz, 133–134; letter on uniqueness (Alicia), 135–139; letters on being self (Peter), 141–145; letter to former new teacher (Pamela), 147–151

Thompson, David, 41–42, 43, 47–48

ticket-to-leave cards, 45

Tomlinson, Carol Ann, 59

tradition, xxi–xxii, 11, 143

training: pilot, 153, 155; teacher, 154–155

Tristan, Rob, 113–116

trust: paradigm, 163, 164–168, 169; student-teacher, 166; in teachers, 79, 99

Tufte, Edward, 115, 117

Tumblr, 57

Turkle, Sherry, 2

Turning to One Another: Simple Conversations to Restore Hope to the Future (Wheatley), 29

Twitter, 55

Understanding by Design (UbD), 54–55, 59, 106

unfolding, allowing student, 123

universe, Internet as, 95–96, 98, 99

valuing conversation, 29–34; Inside-Outside Circles for, 32; principles, 30

visuals, in DI, 53

voice, consultant feedback on loud, 15–17

Wang, Sandra, 34

Ward, Christina, 107

washing dishes mantra, 104, 105, 124

Waters, Adrian, 71–73

websites, 8; DI, 59; lesson posting on, 80; Primacy-Recency, 49n13; researching using, 47; UbD, 59

Webster, Sheila, 120–123

Wheatley, Margaret, 4, 29–34, 37n2

Wiggins, Grant, 19n3, 59

Wilson, Judy, 87

"'The Wisdom of Confucius: As Written by His Devoted Disciples,' Under the Tutelage of Allison-ti," 77–78

Wiseman, Frederick, 159

Wong, Harry, 137, 140n2, 147

word processing, 1990s, 82, 83

writing: to newspapers and blogs, 91; to other students, 91; value of letter, 133–134. *See also* essays; letters

Zander, Benjamin, 9–10, 12

"Zippy the Pinhead," 57

Acknowledgments

I want to acknowledge first those special teachers who, unbeknownst to them, led me to become a teacher and writer. Miss Karasack in the fourth grade, the tallest person in my world then, had patience with my insistence on taking shortcuts; Miss Mason in the sixth, shorter and teary-eyed, allowed for emotion, especially when she read aloud Longfellow's *Evangeline*.

Thomas Donovan, cantankerous and brilliant, challenged me to learn two years of French in one; Charlie Keller, beloved family friend and professor, encouraged me to become a teacher; and two history professors: Orville Murphy first saw my real potential as a student, and Sidney Eisen trusted my abilities at a difficult time that allowed me to stay in college.

In graduate school, Reginald Archambault, preeminent philosopher, taught me to seek my own answers. Later, in graduate school again, Vincent Rogers steered me to Oxfordshire for one of my most memorable years of teaching; Philo T. Pritzkau, archetypical professor of philosophy, taught me and my classmates to see everything as it is.

I am indebted to my first students, upon whose shoulders I began pursuing my dream—and since then to each and every student I've been blessed with, to have taught and learned from. Without students, teachers cannot teach; without mine, I would not have become the teacher I am. And I am especially indebted to three mentors: Delmar Goodwin, Barrie Rodgers, and David Mallery. Creative, persistent, compassionate men.

Now as a writer, I have been encouraged by wonderful people over the years. Many have stayed with me from my earliest efforts. Jill Mirman's advice and counsel has enriched my thinking and supported my ideas. John D'Auria, President of Teachers21, has encouraged my efforts both as a consultant and as a writer. And, of course, my dear friend for the past fifty years, Barbara Barnes, to whom I have dedicated this book.

Many people have commented on parts of the book: Peter Bien, Barnes Boffey, Joyce Barnes, Ursula Boyle, Bud Brooks, Frank Gould, Bob Milley, Liz Morantz, Melissa Matta, Ron Stegall, and Steven Levy. John Maguire critiqued an early manuscript and offered invaluable editorial and writing advice. Ken Morrow, Lynn Learned, Sharon Steeber, and Chet Kozlowski added critical insights to my writing process during the latter stages.

Pam Penna, former consultant colleague at Teachers21, wisely encouraged me to include ideas and strategies that would help teachers incorporate the ideas suggested in the book. Susan Page provided invaluable direction and support in seeking a publisher. Agents Jeff Kleinman and April Eberhardt offered impeccable advice. And my wife, Kathleen Cammarata, has inspired me to persist no matter what—and do everything I can to get it right and move on to the next book.

And I acknowledge Christina Ward, book agent and former longtime editor at Little Brown who let me know that my writing was headed on a good path. It is with deep sadness that she suddenly passed away before this book was finished.

Frank Thoms

About the Author

Frank Thoms is a lifelong classroom teacher, consultant, and writer. He devotes himself to improving the teaching profession to meet the challenge of today's digitally wired, techno-literate students. He advocates that teachers become change makers in their own right. He believes invitations offer the most powerful impetus to affect change, in stark contrast to federal, state, and local mandates that often cause resentment and resistance.

Frank believes that it's time to declare that teaching and learning is not a business, that it does not seek to make a profit and construct a successful balance sheet. It is personal. It's about patience and persistence. It's about supporting students to become who they are meant to become and how they can be of service to others.

Frank has taught in public and private schools in the United States, as well as in schools in England, Russia, and Kazakhstan. He is a founding member of the exemplary Upper Valley Educators Institute, one of the nation's first alternative teacher certification programs, now in its fifth decade.

He developed a model open-education classroom that served as a resource to New England schools. He has consulted for PBS, AFS Intercultural Programs, Boston Area Teachers' Exchange, the Kettering Foundation, Association of Independent Schools of New England (AISNE), and the Vermont State Department of Education.

As a consultant, Frank has served in more than 125 schools, providing keynotes, workshops, pedagogical courses, mentoring, and teacher coaching. His unique style blends serious content and pedagogies in an interactive format that serves as a model for the types of teaching he advocates throughout this book.

Contact Frank at frankthoms3@gmail.com

www.ingramcontent.com/pod-product-compliance
Lightning Source LLC
Chambersburg PA
CBHW052117300426
44116CB00010B/1695